Essential Guide to Lean Six Sigma & Business Improvement

The secrets every leader or manager should know; a practical roadmap to successful cultural and business change through Lean Six Sigma

John Wellwood

Preface

For over 30 years, I have been supporting companies to implement business improvement and change in some shape or form. I have had the privilege of training thousands of people in the principles of Lean, Lean Six Sigma, JIT, Kaizen, Change Management, TQM, etc. Hundreds of companies have sought my counsel on how to implement business improvement, continuous improvement, operational excellence or other titles, in order to engage staff and make a difference to their company and their client experience.

Through all these years, my knowledge and understanding of what works and what doesn't has grown. My advice has changed, been shaped by experience and altered through discussions with everyone I meet. However, my frustration has also grown, seeing companies make the same mistakes over and over again. Watching as leaders and managers seek the silver bullet or the simple fix, reading books and listening to experts say that this or that approach is the only way to make a difference, has become aggravating.

As a result, I wanted to explain to leaders, managers or anyone interested the requirements for success, the pitfalls to avoid and the secrets others are not sharing with you. There is no silver bullet; there is no one size fits all solution to business improvement. It varies company by company, function by function and leader by leader. You must spend the time understanding the principles, all the various approaches, the tools and techniques as well as why some companies will be successful while others will jump from one initiative to another wasting time, money and frustrating their staff.

Your business is unique. Each one has different challenges, different cultures, different people and different goals so how can you use one approach to make a change and a difference? It's impossible. You must design a solution to suit your individual needs. That requires leaders and managers committing time and effort to make the change to ensure your business can become the best it possibly can be. This book has been written to explain to anyone willing to listen that there is no short circuit to success but we can learn from others, understand principles and shape our own destiny. This book doesn't explain the approaches of Lean or Lean Six Sigma; it doesn't explain the tools and techniques associated with business improvement, as many others do. It is written to open leader's and manager's eyes to the key requirements for success. To provide you with 30 years of insight on how to make it happen.

Focus on understanding that business improvement, continuous improvement or whatever you want to call it, engaging staff in identifying and solving problems, anticipating issues and engaging their brains in helping the company is, in fact, a massive change program in your business. This means that it starts with the leaders, the managers and the owners of companies. They must spend time learning, they must make changes in their behaviours, attitudes and approaches. I have lost count of the number of companies who have asked for our support, but when we say let's start with a champion workshop or senior management training day, it becomes impossible to even free up 6 hours of their time to learn what is needed for success. If you can't free up 1 day as a leader or management team, are you really interested in change?

The approach Lean, Six Sigma, Lean Six Sigma, etc. is not the important part. Understanding the tools and techniques is not the important part. It's about a change in attitude, a change in behaviour and designing and developing an approach that will work for your company and your circumstances.

Virtually all the improvement projects we work on or our delegates work on can develop a solution relatively easily, once they have been trained in some basic approaches. However, where they all find it difficult is implementing these new solutions. The same applies to implementing your designed business improvement approach. Why should people at any level in a company change? What's in it for them? Can they do it? Do they want to do it? What motivates them?

How can we influence them? These questions become the real challenges. As such, this book has been written to provide an insight into what is required for success, to teach people what not to do and provide an insight into the key elements you need to consider if you want to make business improvement a key part of your company.

CONTENTS

SECTION 1

Introduction

Every business is unique; each has its own history, culture and objectives and there is no one size fits all solution to implement Business Improvement. All we can do is learn from others, understand the principles and adapt them to suit our needs and wants. Understanding Business Improvement is simple. The difficult part is applying it in your business and ensuring that your people accept it as the way forward so that you can change the culture of your organisation. It's our people, managers and executives who complicate it and most of the time, the solutions to problems are quite straightforward. It's convincing people to change that makes Business Improvement a challenge.

For over 30 years, I have supported businesses large and small all over the world. Each company has asked us to help them become more efficient, to solve specific problems and to change their culture so that they can improve. Some organisations need to change to survive and others want to stay as the leader in their industry or market but they all have one thing in common. They need to engage their people to identify problems, develop solutions, implement them and have everyone accept the changes.

We have trained people to learn the tools, techniques, principles and methods of Business Improvement, no matter what it is called: Lean, Six Sigma, Lean Six Sigma, Kaizen, Just In Time, Systems Thinking, Business Process Reengineering, Operational Excellence, Theory of Constraints, Continuous Improvement, Agile, etc. We have deployed our people to solve problems for companies, coached executives and staff at all levels to understand and design their Business Improvement approach. We have talked at seminars, written articles and put out white papers in an attempt to educate, train and change the way people think and approach Business Improvement. It has been great fun but more importantly, it has been an amazing learning experience.

Now is the time to pass on that learning so that executives, managers and anyone interested in Business Improvement can understand the essential aspects, discover how to deploy effectively and learn the secrets to short-circuiting the process to avoid the same mistakes made by others in the past.

This book will start by ensuring that everyone understands why Business Improvement is essential in every company, industry and sector, from charities and multinationals to corner shops and government. It will then outline in detail the key steps needed to deploy a Business Improvement culture in your company and how to train, educate and motivate your people to be successful. Lastly, we will provide you with the secrets of how to make implementation a success.

This book will not teach you tools and techniques for 2 key reasons. Firstly, understanding the tools is straightforward and there are hundreds of books and training courses for you to learn how to process map or conduct a pilot or work on correlation, etc. Secondly, as champions, executives and managers, your key role is to plan strategies, motivate, engage and ensure that Business Improvement is a success. So, it is far more important to understand how and why to deploy Lean Six Sigma or Business Improvement rather than the intricacies of the tools. Of course, we would encourage everyone to learn the tools but to start with, executives and managers must understand why and how.

Business Improvement is something every company says it is doing but very few actually are. Only a handful of companies have a strategy and true understanding of how to implement a Business Improvement culture to ensure that all employees identify issues, develop solutions and implement them on a day-to-day basis. This book will make you reflect on your level, commitment and engagement in Business Improvement so that you can understand what needs to be done to transform your company. It will shed light on why Business Improvement is essential, no matter your organisation, and show how to avoid the mistakes made by the majority of companies the world over.

Managers, executives and owners must be brave, committed and enthusiastic about wanting to change their companies if they are to make dramatic changes. Don't be constrained by your current thinking and understanding of Business Improvement; take some time to learn what it is, how it can help and most importantly, how to make it a success.

Take the first step to transform your organisation by reading this book and applying the lessons you learn. If you have questions, then please get in touch and ask; we will be delighted to discuss your unique set of circumstances, requirements and questions. Enjoy the book.

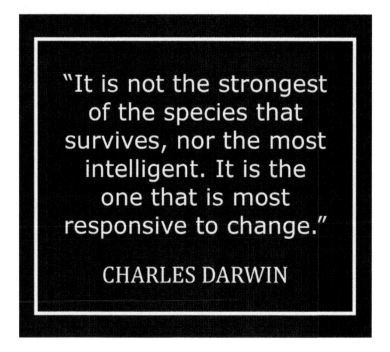

"It is not the strongest of the species that survives, nor the most intelligent. It is the one that is most responsive to change."

CHARLES DARWIN

SECTION 2

What is Business Improvement and why is it essential in any company?

2.1 Why is Business Improvement essential for every company?

Our primary driver as a manager or business leader must be to make our businesses better year after year, day after day. It is amazing how many businesses have no real plan to achieve this, however. You must look at how you can make your business safer, improve customer service, ensure staff are engaged and satisfied, and achieve your company goals. For many, those goals will include increasing profit through increased sales or reduced costs. For non-commercial enterprises, this may be about serving more people but no matter what your goals are, you must understand how to improve your business effectively.

Every company, regardless of their goals, are today facing more and more pressures. Customers demand things quicker at a low price and with more and more functionality and technology. They want to have increased support and customer service but we can't increase our charges. We must embrace the need to save the planet and become more environmentally aware and engaged. International and national laws and legislation make trading harder and harder – just look at Brexit in Europe as an example. The skills gap is widening and obtaining talented people gets harder each year. We must satisfy customers with less and less people due to cost pressures but we must also provide enhanced service. Our staff demand more from us as employers. Our competition is now global, no matter what you sell.

For each business, there will be different pressures or priorities. You will also be able to add unique pressures to the above list based on your situation. However, one fact is consistent across all businesses: we must improve from our current position. If you are the leader in your industry, you need to improve to stay there. If you are anyone else, you must strive to increase sales, satisfaction, profit, etc. It is essential that we all look to improve day by day or we will eventually fail.

Reflect on your current business or a past business you are or have been associated and ask yourself 2 questions:

1. What challenges are/were we facing?
2. Did we have a truly joined-up, communicable plan to improve our business?

Many businesses believe they have a plan or initiative to improve their business but does your whole workforce understand it, engage in it and deploy it each day? If not, then you need to enhance or develop a true Business Improvement Strategy today.

Let's look at some indicators, which will help us understand if we have a plan that is effective. Review these questions to see how well your business is fairing:

- How consistent is your quality? Is every business process producing virtually 100% quality outcomes? Are your products perfect, service exemplary, and your customers getting exactly the same quality of service, no matter which member of staff services them?

- Does every step in your processes provide quality outcomes for the next person to use that outcome so as to ultimately provide your customers with perfection quickly and without rework?

- Can you say that you have no need to firefight? If you can plan your business and its people and resources easily, you won't have to firefight. Is your quality so good and your processes so well defined and adhered to that you never need to firefight?

- How easy is it to plan? Do you understand how long each task takes and can multiple people undertake these tasks with the same quality outcomes? Do you have no tasks where only 1 or 2 people can carry them out, meaning you don't have any risks of people leaving, being sick or going on holiday?

- How standardised are your processes? Is each process only conducted in one way to guarantee quality and service? Does this mean you can train people quickly, assess performance and support them if there are any issues? Can you prove your standards to customers and legislative bodies without any question?

- How do you improve? Is every member of staff looking to identify problems and develop ways to improve every day? How well have you understood and followed processes to identify, develop and implement solutions which anyone in the business can explain and engage in?

- How satisfied are your customers? Do your customers always get perfect products and services and if not, you embrace and use complaints to improve?

- How satisfied are your staff? Do you have a fully engaged staff who participate in the business, are ambassadors for your company and embrace any changes needed?

- Do your Key Performance Indicators drive (KPIs) change? Do your KPIs measure and focus on inputs rather than outputs as you focus on improvements so that outcome indicators such as profit take care of themselves? Do you display your KPIs and the whole body of staff understands them?

I am sure there are countless other indicators to tell us if your Business Improvement plan is effective or not. My experience of delivering Business Improvement over the last 30 years across 5 continents is that most businesses have virtually no plan, a confused plan or a plan which has elements at odds with itself. It is my belief that every business should have Business Improvement at its very core. Every person should see this as a fundamental part of their role in the business.

I would suggest that every person, in particular every manager, should be assessed each year against 2 criteria:

1. How well did you perform in your functional role (purchasing, production, finance, etc.)?
2. Prove how you performed in your business improvement role through speaking with data.

If every appraisal or review focused on Business Improvement as well as traditional elements, cultures would change and businesses would be transformed.

The Hidden Factory or Hidden Business

If you have never heard the term the 'Hidden Factory' before, it may conjure up images of some secret and sordid place. A towering building operated by a workforce sworn to silence, making products that are locked away from the outside world. With this image in mind, you will probably feel uneasy when you find out that almost every organisation has its very own Hidden Factory – even yours.

The Hidden Factory, or Hidden Business, is the work done in our own company that reduces the quality and efficiency of our process: the mistakes, the rework, the waste – all the things we keep hidden from the eyes of the customer. While in reality, these Hidden Factories are not as ominous as the initial image you conjured up, they are still not to be ignored.

All too often, these daily drains on resources are going unnoticed, or are even accepted as part of the process itself. These factories are fuelled by a dangerous attitude that the headaches and heartache caused by this Hidden Factory are surely worth it if the customer remains unaware and is ultimately happy with the product.

These organisations do not understand the dangers the Hidden Factory poses for both the company and its customers.

The Hidden Factory is a dangerous place and as Henry Ford once said, "Quality means doing it right when no one is looking," and if you have a Hidden Factory, you are not doing it right. If you are not doing it right, then you are cheating your company out of its ability to be the best it can be, and consequently cheating the customer out of receiving the best possible output.

No company is agile and efficient under the constraints of the Hidden Factory, and many eventually buckle under the costs of the pretence. Even if your Hidden Factory can survive the pressure of keeping up appearances, with all the best intentions, the deficit costs will inevitably reach your customer.

Finding your Hidden Factory

Finding your Hidden Factory can be difficult; left for so many years, it could be so deeply ingrained in your company that it may even be disguised as your normal procedure. To identify it, you need to ask the tough questions, must be prepared to find the hard answers, and be ready to undertake the trying task of change. This can be scary, but the consequences of ignoring it are much more frightening.

Perhaps you are one of the many companies that have found their Hidden Factory long ago, are fully aware of the waste it is causing, but feel that they simply don't have time to reduce it right now. Well, with most hidden factories taking up 40% to 50% of employee time, it could be argued that you do have the time but are allowing it to go to waste.

Closing down your Hidden Factory

With a Hidden Factory so ingrained in your company, it can be a daunting task to dismantle it. One false move and the hectic process that is currently supplying your customers could come crashing down, revealing your Hidden Factory for all to see. It is for this reason that approaches such as Lean Six Sigma are used.

Lean Six Sigma Belts are trained to identify and systematically shut down hidden factories, and ensure they never restart. Introducing a culture of Business Improvement through Lean Six Sigma is a safe and effective way of deconstructing your hidden business. Guided by a clear structure, driven by data and armed with a wide range of tools and techniques, your team can become skilled architects of change.

UNMASKING THE HIDDEN DEPTHS

Many of the biggest issues in our workplaces are hidden from those who are most in need of seeing them.

Known costs of poor quality

Inspection
Warranty
Scrap
Rework
Rejects

Only **4%** of problems are known to upper management

Hidden costs of poor quality

Lost opportunity
Lost sales
Lost customer loyalty
Cost to customer
More set-ups
Expediating costs
Late delivery
Excess inventory
Long cycle times
Engineering changes
Grievances
Inaccurate or misplaced information
Premium shipment costs
Equipment failures
Unncessary procedures

9% of problems are known to middle management

74% of problems are known to supervisors

100% of problems are known to front-line staff

of problems are **NOT** known to upper management **96%**

Now we have exposed the existence of the Hidden Factory, we must develop a Business Improvement plan to eliminate it.

2.2 Why do organisations not invest in Business Improvement?

There are many reasons why businesses are failing to embrace and deliver real Business Improvement and most of them are the result of poor management and leadership.

Firefighting and a lack of time

I hear this excuse from almost everyone. We never have any time around here as there is always another problem to overcome. We jump from one fire to the next. Many years ago, when I was working for a major conglomerate, my team was tasked to travel the world running diagnostics on each company we owned in each of the 5 divisions to understand what each company's core competencies were. What made them special, what set them apart. Was it technology, was it service, was it a particular product, manufacturing skills, their people, etc.? The idea was that if we could identify core competencies, we could learn from each other or develop new products, markets or ways to improve the whole company.

One of the elements of the diagnostic was to talk to the leadership team in each company and ask them what they thought their core competencies were. Firstly, it was amazing the number of leadership teams who couldn't answer this question. Secondly, after we quizzed and asked them questions, almost without exception, they would proudly say one of their core competencies was firefighting. They said this with pride and then gave us countless war stories to prove how effective they were at reacting to a situation and putting out fires. Of course, this is not a core competency but, in fact, an admission of failure. Failure to plan, to understand your customer, your staff, your market, poor quality, etc.

Most managers get promoted because they can put out fires. They can react and manage a difficult situation; they are dependable in a crisis. Very few managers get promoted because they have no issues due to good planning, have quality processes, have passed on all the skills needed to do their job to their staff, learn and eliminate mistakes, etc. Typically, these people in traditional companies don't stand out. As a result, we promote people who are good at firefighting and enjoy it. They don't like and, as a result, don't value speaking with data, planning, learning from mistakes, taking time to identify root causes to eliminate issues permanently. So, the wheel rolls on.

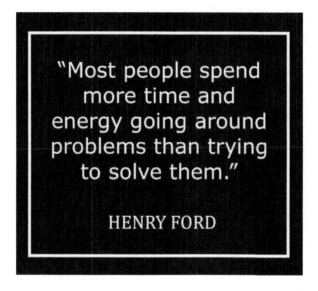

"Most people spend more time and energy going around problems than trying to solve them."

HENRY FORD

We are also told that we don't have any spare people to work on Business Improvement, as if it is a separate element to the business. When senior managers tell me this, I know they just don't get it. Business Improvement is about changing the culture of the organisation so that everyone has it as part of their DNA. Of course you have time; you think about it every day. This is why it has to be part of your appraisal system.

'Everyone is too busy doing the day job' is another common excuse we hear for Business Improvement not starting or being successful. If we work on strategically important elements that need to be improved, why would you not invest your people's time to make things better? Either you don't get it, you like firefighting or you don't understand what Business Improvement is.

Our company structures and KPIs

Although I think this is becoming less of a problem in industries today, we still set up functions rather than think of the world in terms of processes. We have functional fortresses in our business. We are only interested in and measured in how well our function performs. This leads to all kinds of issues. I can succeed but the business fails, however, I still hit all my targets so I'm OK Jack. I may even still get my bonus, pay rise or promotion.

The classic example of this is a manufacturing company I worked with. The purchasing manager hit all her targets and was paid a large bonus. However, when we did some diagnostics, we discovered that they had 5 years' worth of screws, nuts, bolts, etc. in the storeroom. They had saved a fortune by bulk buying and had used this to prove saving and hence be seen as a hero. We then discovered they had done similar things for many other parts. We know for the business this is wrong. Storage costs, the risk of obsolescence, insurance costs, etc. but the way this business was set up meant you only looked after your own function.

When we run process mapping sessions, lots of people in a business are always amazed to know what happens outside their function or what happens to the piece of paper they produce or the report or the product they are involved in. This shows they don't understand the importance of the process and how they affect the end customer and, as result, can't help improve the process effectively.

Quality guru Deming wrote the following statement in the 1980s and it is as true today as when he first wrote it:

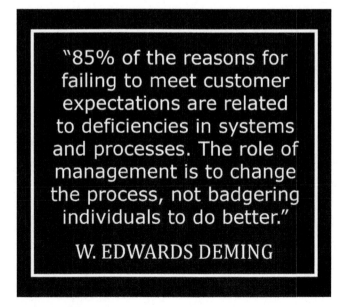

"85% of the reasons for failing to meet customer expectations are related to deficiencies in systems and processes. The role of management is to change the process, not badgering individuals to do better."

W. EDWARDS DEMING

Virtually nobody comes to work to deliberately do a bad job or to sabotage the company they work for. Does that mean that everyone always does a good job? Obviously not, however, the outcomes they get are not deliberate acts. The reasons are very simple: the processes we make them work to are not effective. The systems we make them use are not good enough. This includes our process to motivate, communicate, the KPIs we use which shape behaviour, the tools and resources we provide, the pressure we inflict and the emphasis we place on activities.

Put simply, the structures and KPIs we use in our businesses and the lack of process focus make it very difficult for us to change our cultures to one of Business improvement.

Most of our problems would be improved overnight if we just ensured that our processes and systems were designed to meet customer requirements, were based on best practice and were adhered to by everyone.

If we got everyone in our business to work on improving our processes, we would be better in 24 hours.

Fear of what may be discovered

Another major reason why Business Improvement is not totally embraced in our businesses is down to fear: fear of being discovered, fear of looking stupid, fear of failure, fear of the unknown.

Most Business Improvement approaches which we will discuss later use data to prove root causes, show the scale of an issue and what can be achieved. In a Six Sigma or Lean Six Sigma world, we would use the term 'speaking with data'. Without the data, it is said that it's just an opinion and opinions don't count. In a company where Business Improvement is totally embraced, you must speak with data before making a decision. When you think about it, why would you do anything else?

The answer is simple. Although our businesses collect countless amounts of expensive data, we don't really collect it robustly, understand it or analyse it correctly. Surveys are biased to give the answers you want. We don't pass on data that make us look stupid or weak. We don't even collect data if we don't think we will like the answer. The result is that countless decisions are made every day with weak or no data. I use my gut instinct, it has always been right; this is constantly said, particularly by those who like to firefight.

Data means you must be able to understand it, interrogate it, use statistics. Most managers and leaders can't. Just look at how statistics are used by politicians and in the media. Nobody questions where the numbers come from or asks if they have been collected in the most robust manner; they just use them because they fit their requirements. For most people, Stats is a mystery and for our managers, that is no different. When we provide data to managers, we are always reminded that they don't understand what they are being shown even at a basic level. This means that Business Improvement is not interrogated and used properly.

Managers always fear the unknown and Business Improvement is about investigating the unknown and then finding root causes so you can eliminate them. These root causes are then shared with the company before the solutions are implemented. But what happens if the root cause shows we are not performing, making mistakes or doing something stupid? This is a real fear for many managers and as such, they don't start or block Business Improvement.

Managers also fear that with data exposed, they will be compared with others and so might not advance in the company. They fear that items they have communicated in the past upwards in the organisation might be exposed. They fear they are caught in a lie. All of this fear leads to a lack of control and as such, makes many block true Business Improvement.

Lack of leadership

It is far easier as a leader or manager to focus on operations than to work on strategy or development. Business Improvement is about developing a strategy for your business to grow and advance.

Many managers are promoted on their ability to firefight or their technical capabilities, and this is where they feel confident. As a result, they spend most of their time working in these areas even when they become a senior leader because this is their comfort zone.

A great exercise is to ask yourself or your senior managers the following question: in the last week or month, what % of your time have you spent conducting the following?

- Planning and reviewing and advancing the strategy of the business
- Monitoring, running or checking on operations in the business – day-to-day stuff
- Reviewing the Finances and KPIs and data of the business

When I ask senior managers this question, the normal responses (assuming they are being truthful) would be:

- Strategy – 10%
- Operations – 70%
- Finance - 20%

When you think about it, the operations and strategy numbers are the wrong way around. As senior managers and leaders, our role is to provide the vision and direction for the company. We have other managers and people to ensure shipments are made, to take orders, to check on customers, to check the development of a new product. We don't focus on strategy for 2 simple reasons. Firstly, we have had no training or experience in how to do this and secondly, it's outside our comfort zone so we avoid it.

Business Improvement requires us to think about strategy and then support that strategy. It requires us to perhaps admit we don't understand Business Improvement and therefore acknowledge that we need to spend the time learning about it. One thing I have learned over the years of supporting senior managers in small to multinational businesses is that senior managers never have time. So, getting them to spend a day or more learning about Business Improvement is almost impossible. The result is that they vastly reduce their learning time and then are amazed that they don't support it correctly or they give the wrong message or focus on the wrong elements.

All of this results in Business Improvement not starting or being stopped, as they are not working.

Let's scrap that and try something new – initiative fatigue

Businesses also don't invest in Business Improvement because leaders don't think it is important due to a lack of knowledge or they must be seen to implement something new or they have a misguided feeling that there is a silver bullet that will make everything better.

Let's start by looking at the concept of the silver bullet to make your business dramatically better. There is, of course, no such thing; it all takes hard work, effort and time to make a difference. However, all the major systems companies, consultancies, conferences, books, and technologies tell you otherwise. They are marketed to do just that. Implement SAP and your business will be transformed. Six Sigma saved GE hundreds of millions of dollars so will do the same for you. Automation is the key to reduced costs. etc., etc.

All of them will of course improve your business if done correctly, however, they are not a silver bullet and must be done in conjunction with other elements. No one Business Improvement approach is the right way or the only way (more on this later). A Business Improvement approach must be designed for your business to meet your goals, take into account your history and culture. Nobody should be under any illusion that there is a perfect plug and play solution. That means leaders and managers need to take the time to design the best approach for their needs. All too often, leaders jump from one approach to another as they have been sold by a consultancy or a book or a conference speech. The result is simple: they try half-heartedly for a few months then give up and jump to the next shiny new thing and hope that works. The ultimate result is what we call initiative fatigue.

I have lost count of the amount of companies I have visited when they say things like 'We tried that, it didn't work, don't mention Lean or Six Sigma or Systems thinking around here, it didn't work, that was last year's initiative'. This just shows that you didn't understand what you were trying to implement, didn't commit to it or spend time engaging with it. All of these things are great, you just have to do them properly.

Too often, particularly with new or promoted managers, they have to be seen to try new things, do something to make a difference or establish a name for themselves. As a result, you have to launch something. This leads to failure in the vast majority of cases, meaning Business Improvement is not undertaken properly or at all.

If you don't understand Business Improvement as a senior manager, have had a bad experience (implemented badly) in a past life or want to focus on something else as you think it's the silver bullet, then Business Improvement will not be done.

We don't focus on mistake elimination

Lots of businesses also don't know they have a problem. If you don't collect the correct data or don't understand what to look for, then you would not see the need for Business Improvement. As a result, another major barrier to Business Improvement being undertaken in a business is down to a lack of understanding and lack of data.

Building on the lack of understanding if senior managers don't understand that all mistakes can be investigated and eliminated, then they might just say that it is caused by Human Error. We all make mistakes. However, anyone who works in Business Improvement or has a deep understanding of Business Improvement knows that every mistake should be investigated and eliminated so that it can't happen again. This keeps everyone safe, improves quality, increases customer satisfaction and improves profitability.

2.3 Do I need Business Improvement?

The first thing to look at would be how focused you are on process improvement. As Deming said, to improve customer experience, we should be more process focused. Look at your business; do you see any of the following symptoms?

- Staff work long hours just to complete orders or tasks

- Everyone firefights around the business and heroes are seen as the people who get things done in short timeframes and under pressure
- Planning is minimal and things just seem to get done
- Customer service depends upon who the customer gets to speak to
- The quality of your output varies vastly
- Everything is complicated and complex to complete
- There is lots of rework or completing tasks twice
- There is lots of scrap or time spent on non-value added activities
- When people are on holiday or sick, things start to fall apart or mistakes are made
- Individuals use knowledge as power
- Everything always takes longer than you expect
- As a manager, you don't really know how things are done
- Everything appears to be done last minute

If you have these symptoms, then you need Business Improvement to become part of your DNA – you need to change the culture in your organisation.

Remember, nobody comes to work to do a bad job. Simply asking people to work longer or harder will not work in the long term. Most people already work hard, feel like they are under pressure and are stressed, so adding more on their shoulders will not work.

What businesses have to realise is that we need to improve the process in order to improve the result, not pressurise the employees. Business Improvement is all about switching the focus to the process: reducing waste, eliminating variation, standardising and simplifying.

It uses a structured way to identify and solve problems and vast toolkits to assist us on the way. It ensures the root causes are eliminated so that processes are improved and issues are eliminated permanently.

This is now happening in every business sector, in every business function all over the world and those who don't engage in Business Improvement are being left behind.

It doesn't matter if you work with the end customer or if your job focuses on internal processes with internal customers. Every single process in your business can be enriched, shortened, reduced in cost, improved in quality and ultimately provide your internal or external customers with a better service.

Every process needs to be transformed in our business and as managers that is our responsibility.

Imagine if every person in the company you work in was thinking about business and process improvement each day and had the skills to do it effectively. Even if each person only made a fractional change, the transformation would be unbelievable.

You need to harness the capability, enthusiasm, technical and creative ability of each of your team and funnel that through a Business Improvement approach to make your organisation all it can be.

2.4 What benefits will Business Improvement bring if done correctly?

Any company that successfully implements Business Improvement into its DNA and culture will experience similar benefits. By taking their best people and focusing them on improving the biggest strategic problems in the business, both internally and externally facing processes. While allowing everyone else to make small incremental improvements on a day-to-day basis, you start to see major changes and benefits. Commit your people and allow them time and you will see what is possible.

Solve problems permanently

By attacking the root causes of problems using a proven, structured approach and educating those involved in how to identify and eliminate problems, you can see problems disappear permanently. Traditionally, when we solve problems, we don't collect all the correct data, we don't spend time analysing the issues and as a result, we obtain solutions but they fix the symptoms, not the root causes. Business Improvement done correctly will focus on the root cause, meaning the problem will not come back. This provides 2 benefits. It solves the problem with all the associated benefits but it also means we don't have to waste time solving it again and again.

Solve problems with little capital investment

Organisations using Business Improvement approaches should be able to solve issues with limited capital investment. Typically, the solutions are simple and require little or no investment. The main investment is training and educating your people. This investment will pay for itself hundreds of times over. In a recent Lean Six Sigma Green Belt course we ran for a manufacturing company, one project solved an issue stopping the recall of a series of products. The savings were in the tens of millions of pounds. The training including internal time was less than £20,000 and the solution didn't cost anything to implement apart from some time.

Financial benefits

The financial benefits associated with Business Improvement, Lean Six Sigma and Six Sigma are well documented. Companies such as GE, Motorola and Honeywell have been posting amazing numbers for decades based on Lean Six Sigma projects. Typically, we see projects which on average save around £50K. Projects which save less than £50K either have not had the right support or were not chosen correctly in the first place. We frequently see projects which save well over £100K.

If you put a person onto Lean Six Sigma training and they successfully complete a project, then you would typically expect then to save around £50K. This does depend upon the project. The typical Green Belt or Black Belt will also complete around 3 projects in a year as well as doing their day job, which means that on average, a typical Green Belt will save their company around £150K if they are given the projects and support to complete them. This has to be a major advantage for any company.

Companies can also be confident that the savings are real. This is a result of a key structural element of Lean Six Sigma. The finance department signs off any savings, they say if the savings are real or not. It is no longer just enough for an employee or manager to run a project and say we saved X, Y or Z. In Lean Six Sigma, it is only a saving when finance can see it. A major benefit of Lean Six Sigma is therefore that the savings are real. This gives companies the confidence to say we saved X amount and is why GE and Motorola can publish their savings with confidence.

Strategic benefits

Companies who deploy Lean Six Sigma also see benefits of a strategic nature. This is achieved by taking your trained Green or Black Belt and asking them to complete projects which are of strategic importance – solving major problems in the business. The skillset that a Green or Black Belt will obtain through their Lean Six Sigma training will enable them to solve complex problems for good. They will not just put out fires but they will remove the root causes stopping the fires from starting again. How much time and money have you spent on firefighting over the last year? Lean Six Sigma is about putting out major fires permanently.

As Lean Six Sigma Green and Black Belts are trained to analyse data, they can also assist you in understanding where your current problems are, how large they are and develop solutions to solve them. You can then reassess or develop a strategy for the business based on fact.

People development benefits

The vast majority of people who are trained as Lean Six Sigma Green and Black Belts provide many softer benefits for their organisations. They obtain an amazing amount of self-confidence; the training and being able to speak with data enable them to challenge the norms, suggest new ideas and solve problems. The result of this confidence normally means that Green and Black Belts want to see things in the organisation change and as such, become change agents for the business. If they have influence in the business in any way, then they start to affect those around them to change as well. The result is an organisation that can implement change, develop and grow.

The trained Green and Black Belts also start to understand the need for change in the organisation. They understand and can not only identify but eliminate waste. They start to explain this to other members of the organisation and the business improves without formal projects.

Green and Black Belts also become very enthusiastic about applying the tools and spending time solving problems. They will in fact start to use the Lean Six Sigma methodologies and tools in all aspects of their jobs, meetings and interactions. Your people will have a whole new set of skills to apply in all aspects of their jobs. You therefore see that your people change to become more focused, data-driven and have more energy.

An issue may arise however based on the expectations which are set in the Green or Black Belt. They want to change the business and many become frustrated if the business will not embrace this change. The result therefore can be a highly fired up individual who becomes frustrated, which can lead to many negative consequences for the business.

The benefits to your customers normally take the form of better service, better delivery and even better quality. As a result, many customers are now asking their suppliers if they use Lean Six Sigma in their business. We have clients who have started their programs as a direct result of a request from their customers. So, you can start to advertise the fact that you are using state-of-the-art process improvement and problem-solving methodologies to further enhance your offering to your customers. You can also at that point ask them to get involved and as a result, become closer to your customer.

The immediate benefit to your customers would of course be the result of your Green and Black Belt projects. If you have customer issues, then having a project in that area will dramatically improve the situation. So, if you have delivery issues or quality issues, then your customer will see the difference, meaning at worst, secured continual sales and at best, improved sales.

Competitive advantage

As you improve your performance, you will start to see a difference between yourselves and your competitors. You can then use this in your marketing and sales pitches. On the other hand, if you don't start to implement Lean Six Sigma, you can bet your bottom dollar that your competition either are or will implement Lean Six Sigma. That will leave you trailing them and will ultimately cost the business.

Stakeholder benefits

The key benefit in this area is the engagement of your workforce in transforming your business. Companies that have deployed Lean Six Sigma successfully see this engagement and reap the benefits – the whole workforce identifying and solving problems – how much power would that give you?

It also means you can engage with suppliers and customers to jointly solve problems. Even the shareholders can benefit as many city analysts are now asking why if you are not deploying Lean Six Sigma.

Standardisation benefits

Every company's processes would benefit from standardisation. If you implement Lean Six Sigma, a major benefit would be that all projects would be run in a standardised same way following the same process – DMAIC. This means that, as managers, you can be confident that the problem is being solved properly, with data to back up any decision. It also means that you can monitor the progress of projects easily as you can see which stage each project is in. If you have to change the person running a project, then it is easier for others to pick up where they left off. It also means that your decisions will be based on accurate data, analysis and processes giving improved solutions.

The benefits for any company of implementing Business Improvement are vast when used correctly. Not only will there be financial savings, strategic savings, improved customers and staff experiences but the culture of the organisation will be changed and the attitude of staff transformed. That is why the vast majority of major businesses worldwide are deploying Lean, Six Sigma or Lean Six Sigma in some way.

2.5 What is Business Improvement?

In the last section, we started to mention terms such as Lean, Lean Six Sigma, Six Sigma, Green and Black Belts. Let's examine these terms in a little bit more detail.

Over the last 100 years, there have been a large number of approaches and names associated with making a business improve. Many of these approaches were developed and named by a particular company or person and then others copied and it then became more and more used throughout the world. To give you some examples, how many of the following have you heard, used or read about:

- Lean
- Six Sigma
- Lean Six Sigma
- Kaizen
- Business Process Reengineering
- Total Quality Management
- Just in Time
- Agile/Scrum
- Continuous Improvement
- Operational Excellence
- Systems thinking
- Theory of constraints

I am sure there are a whole host of others. We do not intend to explain each of these terms; a simple Google search will provide you with all the details you need. Having supported clients and businesses all over the world for over 30 years and consulted in almost all of the terms above, one or two things become clear to me.

Firstly, they all have many things in common and secondly, most have been popularised by consultancies, experts and training companies trying to sell a silver bullet.

A company starts to use an approach, be it GE, Motorola, Ford or Toyota, and its people start to see successes. It is natural for us to study these companies and want to duplicate their results. Consultants start to evolve to train or educate us as to how these companies obtained their massive improvements. Eager to find the shortcut to success, we start to deploy these same solutions. Many of us will become advocates of one approach or another. The problem however is that we never really understand why one approach worked well in company x or y. We never deploy it in the same way because we can't. We have different objectives and different histories. The result is we try one way it doesn't work and off we go on the initiative merry-go-round, spending more and more money with consultancies and getting little in return.

However, when you spend time understanding each approach and years deploying them in different industries and countries, some patterns emerge. These patterns start to give us an idea of what can be used in any industry.

Remember, there is no one-size-fits-all approach to Business Improvement. Many people will disagree with this notion and say that Six Sigma is a process and must be followed to the letter as to do anything else means you are not doing Six Sigma correctly. Or that the principles of Lean are the only true ways to implement quick and effective improvements into a company. This is simply not true.

Those that believe there is only one way to do Business Improvement or Lean or Lean Six Sigma leave themselves open to observations such as it stifles creativity, it is only applicable to manufacturing, it can't be used in R&D, it can only be used in mass markets, etc. However, we know from applying it differently that this is not the case. We have used Lean Six Sigma in any industry you care to name, any function you can think of, and for any type of market and obtained amazing results.

The modern take on Business Improvement is that it is a framework, a philosophy, a set of tools, a structure if you like, which helps us solve problems permanently, change cultures, engage people, transform processes and businesses. If we think of Business Improvement in this way, then it will enable us to change the training we deliver, the structure we use and the thinking which restricts us.

We can learn from every aspect associated with Business Improvement (the list above) and apply the elements that will work for our organisation. I really don't care what you call it, as long as you have the key principle associated with it (more below). Call it George, call it quality focus, operational excellence, the name is irrelevant, as long as you are consistent.

Having said that, most companies who are now implementing Business Improvement will use the terms Lean or Six Sigma or Lean Six Sigma in some way. It has become an international standard for Business Improvement. The vast majority of our clients use the term Lean Six Sigma. It incorporates both major approaches to Business Improvement developed in the last 100 years. Lean as developed by Toyota and Six Sigma as developed by Motorola and GE.

Most companies now take a joint approach, applying the learning and best aspects of both. As a result, we will use the terms Lean Six Sigma from now on to mean Business Improvement.

2.6 Key principles everyone should understand about Business Improvement.

When we examine all key Business Improvement approaches, the following principles are key. We do not propose to explain each one in detail. We would suggest that you take a Lean Six Sigma training course to understand each one and the tools associated with them. However, if you understand these principles and embed them in your approach, then your journey to cultural change will have a great chance of success.

Customer focus is key

Every single approach puts the customer at the heart of everything that is done when looking at improvements. This means that our products and services should be designed with what the customer wants in mind. It doesn't mean letting your designers, engineers and marketing people get carried away, putting in features, technology, etc. that will not satisfy your customers. Ensure that everyone in your company understands the concept of the customer. Internal customers are those you pass on any information to, or products, who use your output or services in any way. External customers are the ones who pay the money to the company and regulatory customers are the ones who set or monitor the rules for your industry. Each needs to be understood and studied. Each needs to be at the heart of everything you do, design or deliver.

Ask yourself and your people who your customer is, what is important to them, what their priorities are and how well you are satisfying them. This leads to a deeper understanding of what needs to be improved. A great tool to use is the voice of the customer which we apply to understand the customer in great depth and learn how we can change to improve what we do.

Always speak with data

Taken from a Six Sigma world, this is a powerful way of removing opinions, emotion and management gut feeling from decisions and analysis. Every time a solution, root cause or idea is presented, you should start by saying 'show me the data'. Speaking with data, challenging the data and requiring data will change how people present to you as a manager. It will enable you to make more informed and better decisions. It will mean people and perhaps yourself will have to undertake some training or refresher courses on statistics but it will be worth it.

Quality focus

No matter what activity anyone does in the company, it needs to focus on getting it right first time and quality levels way above your current levels. In a Six Sigma world, people believe that all steps in a process must be 99.9996% good. For some steps in our processes, this is too low; for example, I want key steps in a nuclear plant to be way better than that. For others, the cost of achieving this level of quality is too high. The principle has to be constantly looking to make everything perfect and an aspiration of at least 99.9996% good.

This will mean monitoring all process steps, running improvement projects, educating your people and changing the culture so that OK is not good enough.

Identify and remove all non-value-added activities

Value is anything that your customer would be willing to pay for. If we listed out every single activity or step that takes place in any of our processes, we would see many things a customer wouldn't pay for, such as rework, waiting for information and moving stuff around.

For something to add value, it must change the Fit, Form or Function of what you are buying. In other words; anything that changes its characteristics.

We are also willing to pay for any steps that ensure it is correct or exactly as you expected it to be – that the product is right the first time the customer sees it.

Each of these steps is seen as value-added and everything else is seen as non-value added. Typically, only five per cent of all activities in a business are adding value – the rest is waste.

It's surprising to think that as much as 95% of our processes are waste, but once you start to look at wasteful steps, you understand why.

The eight wastes are known by the mnemonic DOWNTIME and you can review the diagram for an explanation and example of the 8 wastes.

The Japanese word for waste is Muda and they say that when you are looking for waste, you put on your Muda glasses. We want everyone to understand the difference between value-added and non-value-added steps in a process. We want them to see the waste in everything they do through their Muda glasses so they can start to eliminate it. The better your staff understand this, the easier it is to make a massive difference.

A great exercise to do either yourself or with your team is to review a process. Write down every step and ask if this really adds value.

Think about your day yesterday; how much was actually value-added? You will be scared by the results.

Remember that, not all waste can be removed. Some of it is essential for the business to function such as regulatory compliance or inspection and auditing. So, we need to challenge these essential non-value-added waste steps to see if they can be improved.

Standardise every activity in the business to remove variation

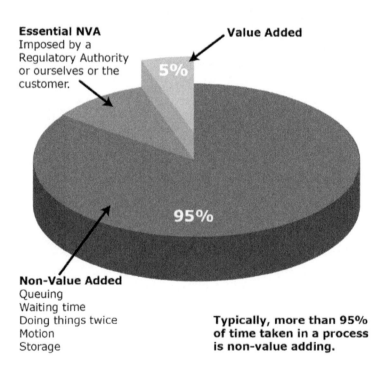

Essential NVA
Imposed by a
Regulatory Authority
or ourselves or the
customer.

Value Added

5%

95%

Non-Value Added
Queuing
Waiting time
Doing things twice
Motion
Storage

**Typically, more than 95%
of time taken in a process
is non-value adding.**

THE EIGHT WASTES

Defects
Work this is less than the customer has requested.

Overproduction
Producing more than the customer needs right now.

Waiting
Idle time, created when material,information, people, or equipment is not ready.

Non-Value Added
Effort that adds no value from the customer's viewpoint.

Transportation
Movement of product that does not add value.

Inventory
More materials, parts, or products on hand than the customer needs.

Motion
Movement of people that does not add value.

Employees (talent)
Not utilising the skills of your people or using the wrong skill level for a task.

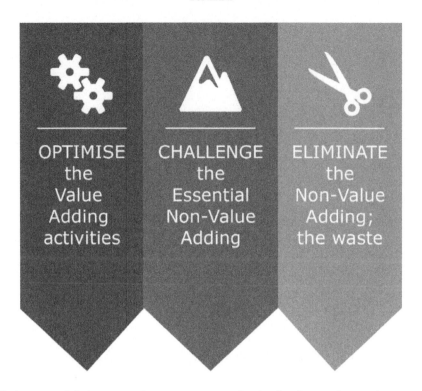

It is essential that we educate everyone in the business that tasks must be standardised. Standardisation is one of the fundamentals of Lean. If we don't have standardisation, then each person does the work in a different way. As a result, the time to do each task is different, depending on who does it, and the quality may vary.

In extreme cases, this can lead to what are called Black Arts: processes or tasks that only one or two people know how to complete. In these situations, the business is very vulnerable to these few people: when they are on holiday or sick, the tasks don't get done until they return, or people try but achieve a poorer outcome in a longer period of time.

Traditionally – and particularly in non-manufacturing processes or transactional processes – we didn't care about how a task was done, only the quality of the output. However, this resulted in poor or loosely-structured processes. Every operator had his or her favourite way of doing the job, which resulted in inconsistent outputs. The speed and quality depended on who completed the task.

This is not a good situation. You can probably think of a call centre, government department or service in your company where the quality of the information you are given depends on who you speak to.

So, what happens in companies where there are no standard ways of working?

- Information is held in people's heads and they can hold the company to ransom
- Tasks take different durations and have different quality outputs
- Customer service may depend upon who helps you or completes your task
- Training is done by the person who trains, which may mean bad practice passed on
- Planning is difficult as you don't really know how long a task will take
- You don't have best practice being used by all
- You can't accurately measure improvement or performance as you don't have consistent data
- If you are off sick or on holiday, it is difficult or takes others far longer to complete tasks

We now care not just about the output but also about the journey to get there. We care that it is done in a consistent manner and also in the best way possible, using best practice.

The goal is that everyone is performing the task in the same way, every single time.

Take Starbucks: Regardless of what you think of their product, no matter which store you go into, the drink you order will always taste the same. Their process is the same everywhere and their staff are all trained to perform them the same way. Their reputation depends on it.

Let's think about what this would mean to your business.

What would happen if from tomorrow, everything in your business was done in a standardised way? What would the benefits be?

- Standards typically save companies money, improve customer satisfaction, reduce lead times and risk in the business
- Everything is done in the same best practice way, leading to consistency, leading to the above
- Customers satisfaction increases as they know exactly what they will get and how they will get it
- Processes are only done one way, making them quicker and, if you use the best way, better
- Training is easier and quicker
- Monitoring performance is easier
- Providing training and coaching for those not adhering is quicker

Why would any company not want to standardise its processes, you may ask:

- If you love firefighting, you would not want processes to be standardised
- If you wanted to be the only person who knows how to do something – makes you important
- You want the power to hold over the organisation or your peers
- You know that people will always come to you and you crave being the go-to guy or the centre of attention
- You don't want to be found out that there are issues or problems

- You don't think others have the capability to do it so will make things worse
- You don't think the way it is standardised is the best way, you might have to change the way you work
- You think that your customers, staff or situation is unique
- You can't see the benefits
- You don't have the time to standardise

As you can see, lots of these reasons are related to the fears we discussed earlier. We must educate and support businesses to ensure that all processes are standardised. If from tomorrow, we did this, the results would be incredible. Think about your business or a business you know. How many processes are truly standardised?

Use a structured approach

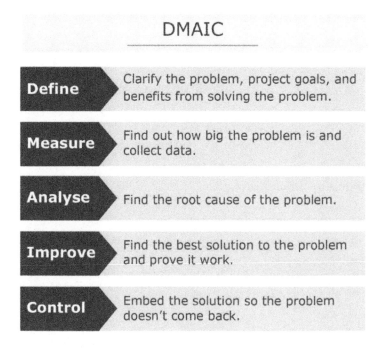

Every Business Improvement approach has a structure to follow to identify and eliminate a problem. Lean uses Plan, Do, Check, Act

(PDCA) and Six Sigma uses Define, Measure, Analyse, Improve and Control (DMAIC). Most organisations now use DMAIC as their structure of choice.

Each of the DMAIC phases has a purpose and we tackle them in a set order because each of them builds on the work that was done before. So, we don't look for solutions until we've found the root cause, and we make sure we know what the problem is before we start looking for causes.

In **Define**, you launch the project by developing a clear project charter and assembling a project team. The team then helps you to understand the needs of your stakeholders and the customers involved in the process.

In **Measure**, you and your team will map the process to understand it, then collect data that allows you to measure how the current process is performing, and help verify root causes in the next phase.

In **Analyse**, you find the critical root causes of your problem by sifting through many potential causes to establish which ones are the most important.

Having found the critical root causes, you then **Improve** the process by selecting the best solutions from a range of options and test the solution before implementing it.

Finally, in **Control**, you make sure the problem doesn't come back by standardising new processes and procedures and putting controls in place. The new, improved process is documented and handed over to the process owner, then the project is closed.

DMAIC ROADMAP

Define	Measure	Analyse	Improve	Control
Launch Project	Map Processes	Analyse Process	Generate Solution	Standardise and Train
Manage Stakeholders	Collect Data	Generate Potential Causes	Validate Solution	Implement Controls
Collect VOC	Calculate Baseline Capability	Verify Root Causes	Implement Solution	Confirm Improvement
Manage Project Risks	Implement Quick Wins			Handover and Communicate Success
Plan Project				Close Project

If you use DMAIC, you will robustly solve problems, it will be difficult for anyone to argue with your conclusions and you will speak with data. It is essential that all Business Improvement projects are run in this way and we should train our staff to do so.

Eliminate mistakes

If we never make mistakes then our products and services will be perfect. However, we all make mistakes; this is just a fact. As humans, we fail from time to time, as managers and leaders, we must look at ways to eliminate mistakes. I am positive that there is a mistake in your business which is made regularly. It might be small, it might not get reported, but it costs time and money, and may lead to customer service issues or worse health and safety issues. You may have tried to solve this issue but it keeps coming back. You have identified that it's just human error, people making silly mistakes or just something

41

solved. I would suggest that it can be solved, it can be
d it can be eliminated.

rrors or mistakes can and should be investigated and
then systems, mechanisms, changes, procedures, checks, etc. need to
be put in place so they don't happen again. Why did we ship that
product to the wrong place, why did we not connect those two parts
together correctly, why did we take that order or booking, why didn't
we complete the form correctly? We need to stop these things from
happening.

Human Error Investigation & Elimination is crucial for every
business. As part of the investigation into a mistake, there is a whole
series of questions and areas to look at. Why not use this basic list of
questions next time you see an issue or mistake in your business. If
you train your staff in Human Error Investigation & Elimination,
then they will understand why humans make mistakes, how to
identify them, investigate them and then eliminate them.

Test this abbreviated list of questions on any mistake you have in
your business. You will discover that it is more than just about
training people, having a procedure and measuring performance.

- Was there a procedure that should have been followed?
- Had that person been trained in that procedure?
- Can you prove that they understood the procedure?
- Had they been told not to follow the procedure? If so, why?
- How much experience did the person have in completing this task?
- Did they have the tools, equipment, materials, systems to ensure that they could do the job?
- Were they motivated to do the job correctly? Is there a consequence to not doing the job correctly?

42

- Was the person under stress at the time of the task being completed?
- How were communications at the time between managers, team leaders, supervisors, other team members around the task where a mistake happened?
- Were other team members exerting peer pressure in some way on this individual?
- What time of the day did the mistake happen?
- Was the individual distracted in some way?
- Is the individual physically capable of completing the task?
- What kind of sleep pattern has the person had?
- Were they eating properly?
- Physically, were there any issues – out the night before for example?
- Is there enough light, too much noise or other distractions?
- How is morale at the moment?
- Is there tension or issues with supervisors, managers, team leaders?
- Was the information given to the individual misleading, confusing or badly timed?

Anyone involved in Business Improvement, Continuous Improvement, Lean, Six Sigma, problem-solving or operational excellence knows the importance of identifying and then eliminating true root causes. Human Error Investigation & Elimination is a key tool to analyse a problem and then develop solutions to eliminate them. Mistake Proofing and Poka-Yoke are just some ways to eliminate mistakes but we need to identify the real root cause first. Learn about Human Errors and you can make a massive move forward in your fight against errors in your business.

12 REASONS WHY A HUMAN
MIGHT MAKE ERRORS

Confusing procedures
Poorly written; vague or superfluous instructions that are hard to follow.

Personal distractions
Personal life; illness; injury; disability.

External distractions
Noisy environment; frequent interruptions; poor layout or workflow.

Procedure inaccessible
Employee unaware of the procedure's existence; inaquequate communication of procedural changes.

Procedural updates
Updates occur too often; procedures released inconsistenty.

Intentional misuse or willful misconduct
Employee is disgruntled or dissatisfied.

Inadequate clearance on automated systems
Another's employee's ID or login is used; unable to access automated systems.

Inadequate paper-based systems
Printer errors; misnumbered or missing pages.

Inadequate software-based systems
Software glitches; unauthorised workarounds.

Employee apathy
Lack of motivation; bored with the job; unaware of the affect on quality.

Missed steps in a procedure
Instructions are unclear or illegible.

Employee unable to perform certain steps
Inaccessible or inappropriate fixtures, tools, or equipment.

Remove complexity/simplify

Over the years, all businesses have added levels of complexity into their products, services and processes. The more technology, the more bells and whistles we offer, the easier it is to differentiate and sell our products. Engineers, designers and marketing teams all love to make our products more complex. However, this comes at a cost. Manufacturing or servicing clients is harder and so it costs more, we make more mistakes, we hold more stock, we scrap more products as they become obsolete, we need more people to manage the whole thing.

Removing complexity by simplifying our designs, offering and activities makes complete sense. Why have 3 different bots in a design when we can simplify it to just 1? Why have 10 variants of a product which are almost the same instead of simplifying to one or two?

American Airlines reviewed the amount of different planes it carried in its fleet. They vastly reduce this number over several years. Why?

- It makes maintenance easier as you only have to carry spares for a few planes rather than many
- It's easier for ground crew when getting ready for a flight as they are familiar with each plane type
- It is also easier for flight crew as they know the layout of the plane
- This is also true for passengers as they know what the planes look like and their layout
- Purchasing can make larger orders for planes and parts as they are only purchasing for a small number of plane types
- The design crew adding seats, etc. will only have a few specs to make their standards seats work in all aircraft
- Etc.

The more we can get each person in our business to think 'how can I simplify everything I do', the better. Instead of filling out 2 screens of data, how can I make it 1? How can I remove this step in the process? How can I automate the filling- in of this field? The list goes on and on. Business Improvement approaches all look at ways to simplify and remove complexity.

THE PRINCIPLES OF HUMAN PERFORMANCE

People are fallible, and even the best people make mistakes.

Error-likely situations are predictable, manageable, and preventable.

Individual behaviour is influenced by organisational processes and values.

People achieve high levels of performance because of the encouragement and reinforcement received from leaders, peers, and subordinates.

Events can be avoided through an understanding of the reasons mistakes occur and application of the lessons learned from past events (or errors).

Common tools

Another key factor when discussing Business Improvement is around tools used to support your efforts. It doesn't matter where the tool comes from or what methodology uses it. There are hundreds of tools associated with Business Improvement. Each phase of DMAIC has tools that make it easier to define a problem, analyse a problem and so on. It is essential that anyone undertaking Lean Six Sigma understands as many tools as possible so that they can effectively solve problems.

The more tools you have used and understand, the better. However, there are some which we would classify as essential for all staff to understand. As the level of the problem being tackled increases, so should the knowledge or the person solving the problem and hence, the tool set should increase.

In a Lean Six Sigma world, we classify this level of complexity into belts:

- Yellow Belts work on day-to-day and smaller improvement projects
- Green Belts work on more complex problems but typically within their own function
- Black Belts work on strategically and cross-functional projects
- Master Black Belts work on highly complex problems as well as coaching and training all other belts.

There are books of knowledge for each level. However, let us share what we believe are the essential tools everyone should be aware of so they can solve simple day-to-day problems.

LEAN SIX SIGMA BELTS

Champion & Sponsor Senior members of the organisation who offer support to ensure the success of the project.	**White Belt** Individuals who have a basic knowledge of Lean Six Sigma, but not enough to participate in projects.
Yellow Belt Project team members with an understanding of key concepts and basic tools. Their role is to assist Green Belts.	**Green Belt** Often management level individuals able to lead small Lean Six Sigma projects. They can also assist Black Belts on larger projects.
Black Belt Operates Lean Six Sigma projects as a full-time role within an organisation. They lead Green and Yellow Belts and can overcome complex problems.	**Master Black Belt** The highest level of Lean Six Sigma knowledge and experience. Often a full-time role mentoring Black Belts and coaching Lean Six Sigma.

Define

When you define your problem, you must write a problem statement to explain the problem in simple terms so that it becomes clear to anyone why this is a problem that demands immediate attention. You must also have a scope so you know what the parameters are of your problem/project.

You must have a goal to aim for so you know when you have been successful, and you need to understand who the beneficiary (or customer) of this project is so you can identify what is important to them.

Finally, you must know the key stakeholders and have a rough timescale for competition. To complete all of these steps, the tools you need are:

- Problem statements
- Scoping diagram
- SMART goals
- Voice of the customer
- High-level goal project planning
- Stakeholder analysis
- High-level process mapping techniques

Measure

We then start to measure how big or small the problem is so that we can assess if it's worth spending some time over. We need to collect data to prove where the problem manifests itself and to be able to show our improvements. To this end, we need to understand a little about data, what it is, and how to make sure it is reliable and accurate.

To start with, we should assess all the data we'll collect and how to do it, so we'll need to understand data collection planning. We also need some fundamental data collection techniques including:

- Check sheets
- Tally charts

Once we have collected the data, we need to display it to ensure the evidence is clearly presented. For this you need:

- Histograms
- Pareto Charts

- Pie charts
- Run charts

Analyse

When we have the data, we then need to analyse it to identify the root causes of our problem so we must understand how to work with a group, facilitate the group and some techniques to generate the root causes. The tools we need for this are:

- 5 Whys
- Cause & Effect diagrams
- Facilitation skills
- Working in teams

Improve and Control

Now we know what the root cause of the problem is, we need to solve it. This involves generating a list of potential solutions, prioritising our list and then implementing our solutions. To generate a good list, you need to work with others, have a good knowledge of how others have solved problems and to be able to think creatively. The techniques we'd use are:

- Brainstorming or brainwriting (putting ideas on post-it notes)
- Affinity diagrams
- How to create simple solutions - 20 questions
- 5S
- Visual management
- How to influence others to come up with ideas

Our long list of ideas can then be reduced to the one or two that will work. It is important to use analysis tools for this, rather than jumping to the first option or going with the boss' suggestion. These are:

- Decision matrixes

- Pareto voting
- Paired comparisons
- Weighted voting
- Payoff matrixes

We can use one or a combination of these tools to come to our decisions. From this point, we can implement them and solve our problem. You need to understand how to identify the savings you have made and how to pass the solutions to others. The last set of tools you need are very simple:

- Control plans
- Saving calculations

The only other things you will need on every project are a project charter – to explain to people at the start what your project is about – and a storyboard to summarise the project overall.

Master these simple tools and you will be amazed at what you can achieve. As the complexity of the problem rises, then you would start to use more advanced statistical techniques as well as more knowledge of how to solve problems. However, these tools are well known and can easily be taught when required.

Safety improvement and risk removal

Every manager should have safety as their number one objective for their business. The safety of staff, contractors, customers and the public. When undertaking any improvement, we must assess what the risks are and how we can eliminate them or vastly reduce their chance of occurring. To this end, this is an unambiguous message which must be sent from senior managers.

All projects must include a risk assessment. When selecting projects to be worked on, any safety issues should be addressed first.

Certification

Lean Six Sigma Certification demonstrates an individual's knowledge, skills and dedication to achieving a high level of competency in Lean Six Sigma. The Lean Six Sigma certification standards require an individual to pass rigorous training and testing hurdles to gain Lean Six Sigma certification.

The issue with Lean Six Sigma certification is that there is no governing body that oversees certification. This is why some people who say they are certified are, in fact, not certified but trained. Any company that says that you will be certified after just attending the training or passing a multi-choice exam is not demonstrating certification at all.

Effective certification requires that a person not only understands the principle and tools but can demonstrate they have used them. After all, I can go online and learn how to play the piano but you wouldn't want me to play at a wedding. You must demonstrate knowledge and application to truly certify.

Certification is important as it demonstrates to the business that you have professionals working on improvement. It demonstrates to your staff you are investing in them and it provides evidence that you have made a difference.

All companies who are serious about Lean Six Sigma will run a robust and effective certification process. This means that to certify as a Lean Six Sigma Green Belt, you must pass an end of course exam and then complete 1 Lean Six Sigma DMAIC project. For Black Belt certification, you must complete 2 projects. You will then have to present your projects to senior managers who will sign off your certification.

As a result, we believe that if everyone in a business is aware of these essential principles then they will understand the key elements to enable them to identify issues and start to eliminate them. Every Business Improvement approach has these principles in its foundations. Today, we use whatever tool and approach works to make a difference. It is a major mistake for any business to take a purist route to improve their business say by only doing Six Sigma or Lean. You need to train your people in all aspects of business improvement.

Do not get convinced that one way is better than another. Don't get hung up on the name for your deployment. Do what works for you, design it to suit your needs and then commit to making it work. As we mentioned, most people are using the term Lean Six Sigma because it encapsulates the 2 main approaches, it is recognised worldwide and as such, trainees qualification have some weight. In Section 4, we will discuss some of the key elements of an effective training program and what makes sense to include.

2.7   The cost of 1 months delay

As we have seen, Business Improvement is vital to every business. However, I am amazed at the number of companies who develop effective solutions to problems but don't implement them or delay the journey to Lean Six Sigma. The cost of the delay in implementing a solution can of course be calculated as outlined below. I feel that if you can calculate the cost of the delay, then you can use this to ensure decisions are made quickly, influence the business to make decisions and ultimately ensure that improvements are implemented.

Delays of course come at different times in Business Improvement. I come across companies who delay the start of deploying Business Improvement while they cogitate the decision. Or companies who think we better spend additional time going out to tender to make sure we have the best deal. Or companies who put off a decision until the next board meeting. Or companies who just find it hard to make decisions.

The results are quite staggering. If you have conducted a business improvement project correctly, you know certain things, including how much it is currently costing you or the impact of the issue on your business in other terms. You will have collected the correct data to prove these numbers and then analysed the data to identify root causes and then generated solutions to eliminate them. It is typically at this point that a business improvement person such as a Lean Six Sigma Black Belt or Green Belt will go to their Sponsor, company board or manager for approval to proceed.

After they have presented their case and assuming that the arguments are accepted and solutions agreed, every day that is lost is in effect lost money, lost customer satisfaction, etc. A good way of saying this is there is a cost associated with every day we don't implement solutions, roll out solutions or take a decision. We call this the cost of 1 month's delay due to the amount of times a business says we will decide at next month's board meeting. Great – that's another £20K lost to the business.

Let me give you some examples of how the cost of 1 month's (or multiple months) delay can affect your business.

I was working with a firm where they had run a Lean Six Sigma project to review the costs, quality and retention of their recruitment process. The result was that they would move to an outsourced solution. The benefits were calculated at £23K per month. When presented to the board, they wanted to go out to tender even though the person had conducted a review. The result was an 8 month delay in choosing the same supplier, that's £184K.

We were contacted by a council 2 years ago about running a Lean Six Sigma Green Belt course for 10 of their people. The cost would have been around £15K. They have still not decided to run the course and come back to us every quarter for a new proposal. When you think that the average green belt saves £10K per project and can run 3 in a year, that means that they have lost conservatively £600K over a decision to spend £15K, even with our guarantee of saving 3 times the cost of the course or don't pay us.

I am currently working with a company that last month delayed 4 projects from being implemented because the board meeting ran over and the business improvement slot was lost. This cost the company £53K, assuming they sign it off this month.

The cost of 1 month's delay is a powerful number. Use it to get senior managers to understand the impact of not making a decision. Use it to influence so you can get resources. Use it to get your training signed off. Use it to communicate the importance of the change you are trying to implement.

Now that you have read this opening section of the book, we would urge you not to delay. Every month you don't plan and implement Lean Six Sigma or Business Improvement will mean thousands of pounds or dollars lost. In the next section, we will look at how to deploy Lean Six Sigma successfully in your business.

Section 3

How to deploy Business Improvement successfully in any company

3.1 Introduction

Every business requires to deploy Business Improvement and as such, needs a plan or strategy to do so. The question is how to deploy effectively: how can we learn from the thousands of other companies that have deployed both successfully and unsuccessfully all over the world? What should be our focus, what should be involved and included in our deployment?

> "Change is the law of life. And those who look only to the past or present are certain to miss the future."
>
> JOHN F. KENNEDY

> "Progress is impossible without change, and those who cannot change their minds cannot change anything."
>
> GEORGE BERNARD SHAW

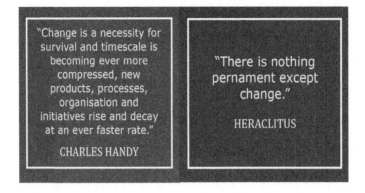

"Change is a necessity for survival and timescale is becoming ever more compressed, new products, processes, organisation and initiatives rise and decay at an ever faster rate."

CHARLES HANDY

"There is nothing pernament except change."

HERACLITUS

3.2 How to deploy Lean Six Sigma effectively in any organisation an overview

There are countless books and approaches to help you understand how to deploy Lean Six Sigma effectively in a business. For the last 21 years, we have supported companies to do just this. As a result, we know what works and what doesn't. This section of the book will provide you with some guidance based on our experiences.

The first thing to remember is that there is not just one way to deploy successfully. It really depends on your culture, your history and your objectives. If you are one of the many companies that have tried numerous times before to implement some form of Business Improvement, then your approach will differ from a company that has never tried anything before.

We often come across companies who say they have tried Lean and it didn't work, don't mention Six Sigma around here – it has a bad reputation. So, we must tweak approaches to deploy successfully based on your history. To that end, we would not prescribe what you call your deployment, where you start or what to include. However, we can provide a set of guidelines or principles which we know work. You can then adapt them to suit your exact needs.

Implementing Lean Six Sigma is a major change program for most companies. The bigger you are, the more this becomes true. Implementing Lean Six Sigma properly takes time, effort and money. It requires that people are educated, trained and convinced of new ways of working, solving problems and how to improve your business.

You must therefore treat Lean Six Sigma deployment like a change program. You will need a team of people expert in change management, as well as experts in Lean Six Sigma itself. For many, this required outside support from training and consultancy companies. However, this is not essential. If you do engage a training company or consultancy, then you must from the start put in place processes to become self-sufficient and remove them from your company as soon as possible.

Change programs will need you to understand the nature of change and the process to follow to make this a success. We particularly like the Kotter Model. For any manager, we would suggest that before you implement any change in your business, you familiarise yourself with the model. So let's take a look at it.

3.3 Kotter Model – Leading Change

Kotter's ideas were based on a study of change efforts over a 15-year period and set out in a 1995 article in the Harvard Business Review. The article identified eight common errors that organisations make when trying to undertake major changes.

He developed his thoughts even further and, in 1996, developed his eight-step process. This is essentially a roadmap for organisational change, with a strong focus on leadership.

In his book *Leading Change*, Kotter makes an assumption that given the right process and the right leadership, change can be planned and managed. Kotter identified 8 steps as essential to implement change in any organisation.

intained that following the steps would lead to positive change
lling to complete or skipping steps would negatively impact the
chances of success. Over the years, this model has been used with
great success in hundreds of organisations but also by Green Belts
and Black Belts implementing change in smaller aspects of an
organisation. The principles are the same; you just apply them on a
smaller scale. Below you will see the 8 steps identified by Kotter.
Understanding each step will provide you with the knowledge to
implement change in an organisation.

KOTTER'S EIGHT STEP MODEL

 Step 1: Establishing a sense of urgency

 Step 2: Creating the guiding coalition.

 Step 3: Developing a vision and a strategy.

 Step 4: Communicating the change vision.

 Step 5: Empowering broad-based action.

 Step 6: Generating short-term wins.

 Step 7: Consolidating gains and producing more change.

 Step 8: Anchoring new approaches in the culture.

1   Establishing a sense of urgency

If people in an organization are going to change their behaviour, attitude or performance, they must first understand why. If staff believe that everything is going well, they will resist the change as they'll consider it unnecessary. Organisations need to be honest with their staff and share the crisis.

However, all too often staff are unaware that there is any kind of crisis or reason to change. What they see and hear then doesn't match up with what they are told when there is a crisis. If we don't share true performance data and how we compare with competitors with all of our staff, then how can they know there is an issue? If we are buying more and more assets that are not seen as essential, then there can't be a crisis. When managers talk to staff, they say everything is going great, there are no problems and it's all just happy talk then there can't be any issues. If at any time, anyone tells the truth or puts their heads above the parapet and they get shot down, then nobody will tell the truth. If the way we are measured doesn't highlight issues or we don't get honest feedback, then again, we will not see any problems.

As a result, when people are told there is a problem, they just don't believe it or can't reconcile what is being said with what is really happening. We need to be honest with people so they are ready to help the organisation to change.

Change typically takes place when there is a catalyst. Something happens to force the change or for us to take things seriously. This could be a variation of things, from new competition to the loss of major customers or new legislation to price pressures.

It could be that a new CEO arrives and wants to make their mark or has been asked to turn around performance. It could be that you have conducted a diagnostic of your business and identified a major issue. Whatever the reason for the change, you must get everyone to agree to the need for change.

If we can't get the senior managers to agree to the need for change, then we will struggle to make improvements later on. Below are just some of the reasons why people struggle to agree there is a need for change:

- There is a lack of understanding of what is really happening
- Lack of robust data to demonstrate what is happening
- Fear of being found out/discovered/we are not up to the job
- Politics
- Personality clashes
- Lack of energy/motivation to change
- Different measures of performance
- Different understanding of what can be achieved
- Not convinced by the arguments made that change is needed
- Different personal and business priorities

The most common reasons are the lack of understanding about the real threat to the business if change doesn't take place. This is effectively down to a lack of adequate data.

As we move through the list, we can see the gambit of human emotions and flaws. Remember that all businesses are made up of people, and people do not always behave logically, but that doesn't mean that their fears and concerns should be ignored.

Once you have worked out the need for change, we must convince the organisation that there is a level of urgency in addressing the threat.

This is where many organisations go wrong: they spend time convincing each other at executive level but don't invest any time convincing the majority of the workforce. You must make sure you plan your communications, deliver the message effectively, and then listen to feedback. It is essential that you get everyone in the business on the same page, working in the same direction and trying to improve your situation.

If we don't all understand the need for change, then chaos ensues in an organisation. We get senior managers fighting and trying to pull the organisation in different directions. We have a workforce that doesn't understand why all this change is happening, leading to resentment, fear and frustration. This can result in good people leaving the company. And, ultimately, the change fails and perhaps so does the business.

We can only really say that stage 1 is complete when virtually everyone in the organisation understands and accepts the need for change; Kotter was very strong on this point. His findings showed that to be effective, at least 75% of the staff and all the senior management team need to understand the sense of urgency and that change is required. That is, asked why we need to change, everyone provides the same answer particularly, the senior executives in the organisation. This level of understanding is very difficult to achieve but Kotter identified that if time and effort are not put in at this early stage, then success is far harder. Effectively, the foundations for the change have not been put in place.

Here are three questions that will help you understand how to complete Kotter's 8 steps. In any change you are looking to implement, these 3 questions are a good place to start. Why not think about how you can implement Lean Six Sigma in your business and answer these questions:

1. What is the need for change/the sense of urgency in your business?
2. What will prevent people in your organisation from understanding or agreeing to this sense of urgency

3. How will you convince 75% of your staff there is a need to change?

2 Creating a guiding coalition

To be successful, you need to build a coalition, or team, that can make effective change happen. The coalition you develop needs to be made up of the right people, which typically means the executive team with other strong managers and influencers from throughout the organisation, not just senior executives. Consider those who have a strong voice or influence on the workforce; this could include Trade Union representatives or employee representatives, change managers, key workers or experts from your staff, as well as managers and executives. The broader your coalition the better, as you are obtaining buy-in and expertise from the start.

In order to be effective, your coalition needs to be made up of the right people: people who carry authority and influence and who are capable of engaging the workforce. You need to create trust and develop common goals.

Kotter highlighted that this group of people will be your key influencers at all levels of the business and as such, must be a team driving through the change in the business. This means we need people who have energy, drive, are seen as influencers, are leaders, are listened to and respected, have change management skills (or are willing to learn them) and varied experiences so as not to be blinkered.

Trust must be established in this group through the sharing of data, open and honest discussions and working together for the common good. By developing common goals which are agreed upon, the coalition can be a success.

You will know when you are ready to move to step 3 because you will have an effective team with common goals. You can disagree when you are together but show a united front and never question each other in front of others. Change is hard and the best way to get it is to have strong leadership.

Another set of questions to help you think about and plan your change:

1. Who do you think needs to be and should be in your guiding coalition?
2. How will you get this group of people to work effectively together?
3. How will this team show a united front to the organisation?

3   Developing a vision and a strategy

When a change is on the horizon, it is helpful for people to have a clear vision of what to expect and what they're aiming for. This vision should connect with them logically and emotionally so that they feel invested in making the change a reality.

According to Kotter, a vision is, *"A picture of the future with some implicit or explicit commentary on why people should strive to create that future."* Excellent leaders and managers should be highly effective at not only developing visions and strategies but communicating and engaging others to want to strive to achieve them.

So, a vision needs to be:

- Imaginable – conveys a picture of what the future will look like to all levels
- Desirable – appeals to the long-term interests of employees, customers, shareholders and others who have a stake in the enterprise
- Feasible – comprises realistic, attainable goals

- Focused – is clear enough to provide guidance in decision-making
- Flexible – is general enough to allow individual initiative and alternative responses in light of changing direction
- Communicable – is easy to communicate and can be successfully explained within five minutes

It is essential that you take people with you on your journey and that can only be achieved through engagement, communication, providing a sense of where you are going and how you will get there.

Your guiding coalition must develop a clear vision and then every action, conversation, communication must back this up.

When we are developing our vision and strategy, we need to spend lots of time understanding our people. A stakeholder analysis is essential, so everyone involved in the coalition must have a clear understanding of what this is and how it is done effectively.

We need to understand who will be affected by change, and in what way. We must also understand why people resist change so that we can overcome this resistance. The more knowledge you have of change management, the easier this step will become. We would recommend that you have a qualified change manager leading your change initiative.

Think about the following questions when developing your vision:

- What are your objectives and goals for the change?
- Who will be affected by the change and how?
- What is important to each person or group of people?
- How will people react to the change?
- What would make people change behaviours?
- How can we get input from more people to help shape our vision?

- How can we make our change positive even in the darkest of changes?
- How can we paint the picture so everyone can understand it and engage in it?

To complete step four of Kotter's 8 steps, we need to have a compelling and engaging vision of what the future will look like. This should be motivational and clarify what is going to happen.

Our strategy must address fears and influence behaviours, as well as delivering normal action and project plans.

4   Communicating the change vision

The real power of a vision is unleashed when most of the employees have a common understanding of its goals and direction. To that end, step 4 is about communicating the change vision you've developed with your coalition. This is not an easy step and we see countless companies make major mistakes with their communications.

If you don't communicate well, people stop listening and then they stop doing what you've asked and ultimately your change fails. Poor communication of the vision leads to everything taking longer as you have to go over things again and again. You have to constantly be convincing people that change is needed and that your vision is the way to go. People also make the wrong decisions when they have a choice, not deliberately, but because they don't understand the correct route to follow.

If we have inconsistent messages from different managers as an example, then the whole program will stall or stop. Employees will be led by their managers so if they say one thing but the business says another, then they will be in a state of confusion causing real issues in any business.

Another issue with poor communication is that people don't like change, they don't like doing new things outside of their comfort zones. As a result, if they can avoid doing it, they will. Don't give them the excuse to take the easy option through poor or confusing communications.

Lastly, we see lots of confusion and frustration when messages are not clear. Responses like, 'I didn't know that was happening or why I had to do this or that, how did I know what you meant, that's not what XYZ said, nobody asked me', are all common symptoms of a poorly communicated vision.

Listed below are some key elements to make your communication effective. Getting this right will make your whole change programme easier. Use people who are good at communication in your business to help you design a communication plan. This is not a book about how to communicate effectively but let's look at a few tips.

- Repetition – Messages need to be repeated time and time again for them to really sink in. Find different ways to repeat and repeat it. Start every meeting, conversation, broadcast by explaining why and how the change will take place, what is in it for them and how it will affect them going forward. Remember that good communication is designed for the people receiving the message not to make it easy for those delivering the message, which is what is frequently done.
- Quick explanations – A good vision should be communicable within 5 minutes. It should be understandable and engaging. If you can't communicate it in a short time period, keep practising and honing those explanations.
- Language – Everything you say should be framed positively as you are painting a picture of the positive future. Ensure that negativity is not part of your communication of the further vision of the company. If it is, why would I want to be part of it? Language also needs to be used which is easy to understand and again, tailored to your audience. Use pictures, think about

translations, think about acronyms and the level of words used. It's about convincing people so don't make it harder than it needs to be.

- Simplicity – Keep it simple; the words used, the message, the images, the questions. Remove all jargon and technical speak; always assume people don't know something rather than they do.

- Lead by example – It is vital that senior managers and anyone in the coalition walk the talk. They must demonstrate through their actions the new vision. They must make decisions based on new behaviours. They must not be seen to waver from the new path. If they do, people will see this as a way out and your change will be damaged.

- Multiple formats – Good communication means hitting all the senses. It means using different formats so that everyone is captured and engaged. This might mean running mass meetings, one to ones, small group meetings. It might mean developing websites, posters, campaigns – anything that will engage your workforce. This is where a good communications person should come into their own, using different channels to get the message out.

- Feedback – Listening to others is vital to influence them but it also is the best way to get new ideas or understand areas you didn't think about. It also shows that the people you are communicating with matter and that you take account of their ideas, fear and concerns.

- Timing – Think about what time of day or even the day of the week you make announcements. People need time to discuss and digest your vision. Making announcements at the end of the day or week means less time to discuss. This might be easier for those making announcements as they can't be asked questions but it doesn't help our change program. You also need to think about how much time you will give for questions, for people to feedback thoughts and inputs. Announcing something on a Friday which will happen on Monday is not effective. It might be you have to communicate weeks in advance to obtain buy-in, answer questions and obtain effective feedback to help you tweak your ideas.

- Metaphors, analogies and examples – A picture paints a thousand words they say. So use metaphors or analogies. Give examples, take people on trips to see others doing the new behaviour. Use images all the time in your communications but be careful that they send the right messages.

- Dynamic and engaging style – Ensure that the people delivering the communications are engaging and dynamic. This might mean that the leader or senior manager shouldn't do the presentation. It might mean that you don't let them be involved. If they are not the right person, don't put them front and centre of your communication. Remember that this is a vital step in your change program so don't let a boring person derail it.

- Different messages, same theme – Don't use the same communication or presentations for each group of people you talk to. It can't be the same as each communication needs to be specific to the person you are addressing. You need to answer their personal concerns, you need to pitch it at a level they will understand. It is easier to use the same message for all levels and groups in a company but it is a sure-fire way to make your communications fail for all.

- Answer the unasked questions – As you communicate, people will have questions that they may not articulate. If you can answer these questions before they have to ask them then it shows you really understand what is important to them. It means you have taken the time to look at what this means to them personally and you understand their circumstances. Think about what people will ask and help them to understand.

Step four is all about communication; you'll know you're ready to move onto the next step when you know everyone understands the vision and is ready for change. You have told the message in different ways, multiple times, listened to feedback and made changes.

Think about your change program and these questions.

1. What have you tried to communicate in the past and what went wrong?
2. How will you communicate effectively?
3. How will you collect and use feedback?
4. How will you know if your communications have been successful?

5   Empowering broad-based action

Step 5 in Kotter's model is empowering employees for action. Create the conditions to make it possible for people to act without fear, confusion or contradictory consequences. This step is about examining your organisation in line with where you want it to be and removing the obstacles.

For successful change, people must be confident that they will not be punished for making mistakes, trying things or questioning things. This requires that we empower them, support them and encourage them. We must start with a group of employees we think will have influence and the ability to affect change and train and coach them to make a difference. This requires that you set them free to make a difference and that all of your systems and structures support their efforts. They can't be constrained by the very people and processes that caused the problems in the first place. Change reporting lines and workload to enable them to be successful.

In order for employees to start embracing the change and taking actions to move towards the new vision and change, you need to make sure that they are not inhibited by anything in the business.

Typically, this means the guiding coalition reviewing the business and changing things to facilitate the change.

- Adapt the structure – reporting, functionality, hierarchy – If we report to the wrong people, or to people too low down in the organisation, or if your function's requirements are contradictory to the new process, we need to tweak it. Don't let old structures constrain the new approach.
- Ensure consistency of objectives, measures – If we have objectives or measures which push us one way and a vision that goes another way, then we'll be pulled in two directions. Make sure that this is not the case and that everything lines up with the new vision.
- Competencies – identify required skills – One of the biggest barriers to change is a lack of skills needed for the new world. We need to identify the required skills and then train and coach people to obtain them. Remember that this might be behavioural skills as well as technical skills.
- Equipment – computers, tools – Without the right tools for the job, we can't be expected to improve or change. Assess what is needed and then make sure it is available. If not, change will be slowed or stopped.
- Assign responsibilities that are possible – Make sure that if we allocate a responsibility to a manager, they have the capacity, willingness and understanding to succeed. Give the job to the right people and support them so they can manage and motivate others effectively.
- Motivation and support – Investigate how you motivate staff and ask if this approach will support the change programme. If not, then adapt or change the way motivation is tackled.

Think about how you will empower your people to engage with the new world. Plan it and implement these changes and you will start to see people adapt to new ways. Here are some ways to start to engage and empower your people:

- Involve them in the design of the vision
- Let them tweak or adapt the vision
- Communicate from their perspective
- If they make a mistake, support them
- Stand up for them when required with everyone
- Listen to their feedback and react to what they say
- Let them try things even if you think they will fail. If they do, don't say 'I told you so' or 'I knew that would happen'
- Provide them with the tools for the job and the time to do it
- Provide training, coaching and support
- Manage them appropriately
- Ensure they buy into the change vision by working with them until they do

At the end of step five, we should see a few things happening, starting with people at all levels of the organisation showing signs of change. We should see a rush of people to be involved. This is normally the same group of people who support all your new approaches so embrace them but look for those who might not always be the volunteers and engage with them in particular. People will also start to change their language from 'this will not work' to 'I think this will help, make things better and I want to be involved'.

6   Generating short-term wins

As our plan starts to be implemented, the next step in Kotter's model is generating short-term wins. Short-term wins provide a boost to the change initiative. They help to manage negativity and promote support for the change. Wins always provide us with momentum, no matter what we are doing. Seeing successes, people we know embrace and engage and enjoy a new process, which will encourage more and more people to get involved. It will demonstrate more than any words that it will be worth the change required. If you are trying to obtain improvements with your change, it will also provide funding to keep financing your change program, meaning you can celebrate and move to the next area. As you go on, these first projects and wins will provide invaluable feedback about what to communicate, what works well and how to improve. It enables us to learn.

Quick wins are vital for any change program as nothing breeds success like success.

Quick wins are essential to keep momentum but how do we find them? When picking an area to work on or improve, we must select something which will be meaningful to the masses. It shouldn't be so simple that it could easily be solved with just a little attention, but neither should it be so large that it's not feasible.

Instead, study the business and look for wins where you will get a great story or case study or, more importantly, where the changes can be clearly seen and experienced. There is nothing more powerful than that of a change programme! It's even better if you can convince some key players of the benefits at the same time.

Our first changes must be a success so don't leave it to chance. Spend time selecting the area, people and the change agents to make it work.

To achieve success at this step, you need to have completed a number of things. You will have some meaningful results you can share across the business and elsewhere, a case study, data, etc. You will have some real advocates for change, perhaps even some people who were doubters to start with. You will have overcome some resistance and learned how to persuade and engage in going forward more effectively. You will have feedback enabling you to learn and adapt your approach.

7   Consolidating gains and producing more change

Step 7 in Kotter's model is to consolidate gains and produce more change. After the initial quick wins, it is important to consolidate and move the change forward. There is always a pressure to revert to old ways; sustaining and embedding the change requires ongoing effort over a long period. You must embed the change by keeping the guiding coalition engaged, ensuring they don't allow people to use old processes or behaviours. This takes effort as at this point, you may feel you have done the hard work and that you can move to a new activity – you can't. This is when you must stay the course and up the engagement and reinforcement of the new ways. The guiding coalition must be highly visible and keep up the hard work.

Strong leadership is essential to successful change; without it, the staff are unclear of the direction they should be moving in. While it is easy for leaders to lose focus as the change is happening, businesses that are successful do not allow that to happen and do not reallocate resources.

Leadership is vital to ensure

- No loss or resources or budget
- Resistance is fought against
- Additional help is given if required
- The distribution of roles and responsibilities at all levels of the organisation is required
- A reduction in unnecessary interdependencies on change agents or experts occurs so that changes can be run by those who will run them day-to-day.
- Additional and big projects are tackled, rather than just quick wins
- Training and support are in place for all
- The promotion of the change and the communications of successes continue

Without the strong leadership, it is too easy to slip backwards and waste all the effort.

If we are successful in step seven, we should see these things happening within our business. Our KPIs will start to show improvements, we will hit our goals. People will start to see the new ways as the norm. Other improvements will just start to happen without you really being involved and you will have more and more success stories.

8   Anchoring the new approaches

The last step identified by Kotter was to anchor the approaches in the culture. Over a period of time, we will see that our change has occurred and has been embedded in the organisation. We will notice that the culture is different to when we started.

If you compared the company before and after, you'd notice differences in the processes and procedures but more importantly, you'd see them in the way people behave. They have a different language, a different attitude and different approaches. The atmosphere has changed and what is considered the norm is not what it was.

To make the culture change, we must work over a long period of time. We must not forget what the old culture was like and celebrate the differences.

Summary

Kotter's original thoughts and observations were based on organisational change and he developed his model from this perspective.

But over the years, the model has been used by different people in different ways. To make changes across an organisation, within a function, to deploy a project or to implement small change in part of a business.

The thing to remember is that, no matter how big or small the change is, all eight steps must be followed and the role of leadership and communication is crucial. Kotter's model provides us with the basis to implement Lean Six Sigma effectively into our organisations. It is vital we use this knowledge as well as the experiences of thousands of other companies to implement successfully.

3.4 What questions are we always asked when a company wants to deploy Lean Six Sigma?

As we have seen, we all want to implement a culture where Business Improvement is the norm; where everyone engages in identifying problems or issues and then solving them permanently. Over the years, we have worked with hundreds of companies from almost every industry to support them to deploy Lean Six Sigma. At the start of the journey, we are typically asked the same questions:

- What is an improvement culture?
- Why do it?
- How do we change the culture?
- How do we maintain the change?
- How do we go about implementing the change?
- Where do we start?
- What are the pitfalls?
- What structure do we need to implement?
- What systems do we need to use?
- How long will it take?
- What resources will we need?
- What level of training should we start with?
- Who needs to be involved?
- What tools or approach should we use?
- Will we be done in 6 months?
- Can the people trained do this as part of their day job?

- We don't need to train people in x,y,z, because they are already experts or trained in that area
- Do we really need to involve senior managers and if so, can we train them in a few hours?

Using Kotter and our own experiences, we have developed an approach to support a successful deployment of Business Improvement. It takes into account how to be challenged around the change of culture into one of Business Improvement of Lean Six Sigma. Let's look at this and how it answers the questions most commonly raised by clients.

3.5 Deploying Business Improvement

Our approach encompasses five key stages of activity. Let's look at them in turn.

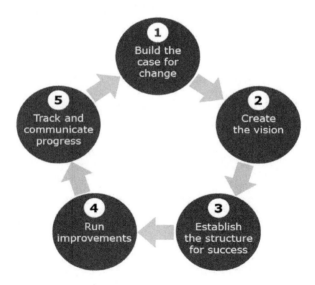

Step One: Building the case for change

Businesses across the UK and the globe are facing unprecedented pressure. The instant gratification culture has led to a customer base that demands more from its service providers. They want a better service, but they want quality to remain high and they want it all without delay.

At the same time, organisations are still facing financial constraints from economic uncertainty and increasing global competition. Businesses that have seen their margins squeezed since 2008 have already identified all of the low hanging fruit, forcing companies to look harder for ways to cut costs in order to deliver the improvements customers are demanding. In the UK, organisations are seeing less money available to invest, increasing legislative and administrative challenges, a dearth of talent resulting in a constant pressure on capacity, resources and time. This pressure is exacerbated for SMEs, which often face the additional burden of cash flow bottlenecks.

Indeed, our own research reveals that 90% of businesses polled consider improving customer service to be one of their highest priorities for 2014, followed by 85% focusing on increasing profits.

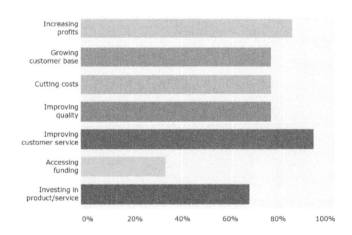

What five key areas are a priority for your business in 2014?

How this shows itself

These challenges are faced by all organisations, irrespective of size, and they tend to be present as specific symptoms. Businesses facing these pressures can find that there is a culture of firefighting; that quality is secondary to getting the task done. Pressure on time forces people to find their own way of performing a process, causing variation, mistakes and often creating a situation where work cannot be completed if an individual is absent.

Training and improvement are put on the back burner as there is no available resource to review existing processes or identify potential cost savings.

Most organisations will experience these symptoms at some point, but many fail to take corrective action because the challenge looks too large to overcome. Instead, a common strategy is to dismiss it as a phase that will pass, and the business will once more begin to improve. However, while ignoring each symptom on its own might not be a disastrous decision, companies that ignore the warning signs risk sleepwalking into a perfect storm of poor customer service, low morale and sluggish sales.

How Business Improvement can help

Business Improvement methodologies provide organisations with the tools they need to put their company back on the path to success. The core benefits to businesses are time and visibility.

With a focus on data, business improvement methodologies such as Lean Six Sigma provide organisations with the information they need about their company to begin to make great decisions. Companies are provided with a clear baseline, providing them with a view into how the organisation is currently performing, but also a benchmark from which to measure future success.

This increased visibility also highlights where resources are being wasted, so that employees have more time to focus on customer service and quality. Lifting time pressure from staff and providing them with the power to implement change engages and empowers them, reducing frustration and boosting morale.

As bottlenecks and blockages are removed, productivity and quality improve, leading to clear cost savings and reduced risk. As a result, companies are reinvigorated, staff are happier and customers are more satisfied.

Identifying your true starting point

While Business Improvement implementation can help, there is a lot of work between deciding to deploy Lean Six Sigma and the first day of implementation. Businesses first need to get a baseline of how the organisation is performing now, and how receptive the culture is to Business Improvement.

Company leaders should ask themselves about the level of firefighting, the volume of customer complaints and the amount of overtime currently essential to get tasks done. From there, barriers and risks to Business Improvement need to be discussed and goals set.

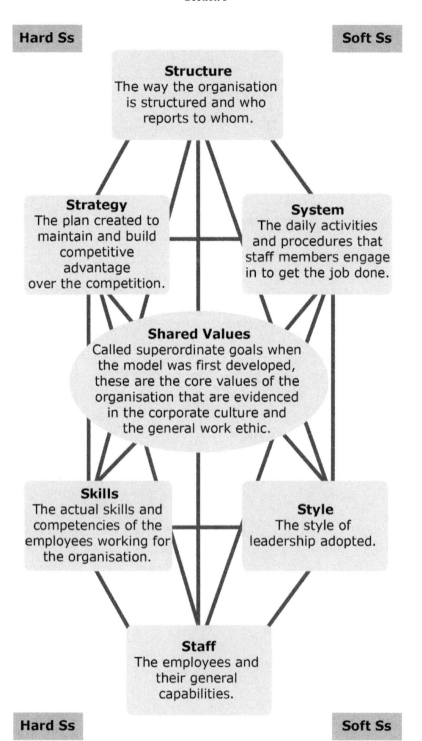

In effect, anyone looking to build a case for change must start to speak with data. They must conduct a diagnostic of the business so they can show the true starting point. There are countless books about how to conduct a diagnostic of your business. Perhaps you could use the McKinsey 7S framework to understand each part of the business or other models. Either way, you must understand where the business is weak. You must also look at the competitors and the market threats and opportunities using a SWOT and PESTLE analysis. No matter what you use, you must be able to start getting people to understand the sense of urgency in the business.

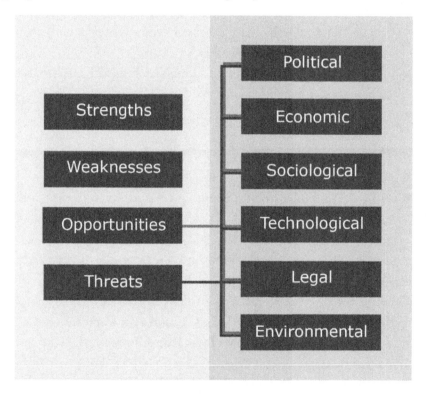

It makes sense to also ask yourself about these types of areas and behaviours:

- Are we constantly firefighting, working long hours, lots of overtime – how big is the hidden factory?

- Do we have a lack of standardisation – no 2 people do things the same, the wheel is constantly being reinvented?
- Are customers at the heart of everything people do?
- Is quality as important as getting the task completed?
- Do we have certain individuals who, when they are on holiday, means some things can't get done?
- How often do we make mistakes?
- How easy is it for us to plan?
- How many people in the business really think about how to make the business better?
- Do we ever find time to think or change or reflect?
- How often do we think about how to reduce costs, apart from putting pressure on our suppliers?
- Do we really speak with data and make decisions based on data or is it just gut feeling?
- Is customer service consistent or does it depend on who is involved?
- Do we have documented and followed internal processes?
- Are we a process-focused company?
- Do we train our staff enough and is training given priority and focus?

The more we can analyse and understand our business, the easier it will be to develop our case for change. Remember, however, it is not uncommon for there to be resistance to change; for employees to warn about a lack of time, funding and resources to dedicate to Business Improvement or for staff to appear unmotivated. However, businesses should not be asking themselves whether they can afford to change, but rather whether they can afford not to. Here are some of the key questions and considerations:

1. How many of your processes are truly standardised so that everyone does them in the same way?
2. How much time is wasted in each key process?

3. How many tasks do you have where only one or two people know how to do them?
4. How many customer complaints do you have?
5. How much overtime and extra effort is put into completing your tasks?
6. Would you say you are great at firefighting?
7. Is there internal frustration at not getting what you want from other staff members?
8. In the last year, what % of staff have suggested ways to improve the business?
9. In the last year, what % of staff have suggested and implemented improvements?
10. How well does each level in the organisation understand the importance of BI and how the business is deploying?
11. Is Business Improvement a key measure for every person in the business? What % of staff have this as a measure?
12. Is there a clear and understood process for suggesting, investigating and implementing improvements in the business?
13. Is Business Improvement a stated goal of the business?
14. If so, are these goals cascaded and visible for each function and level in the business?
15. Does the agenda for board or very senior management meetings feature Business Improvement matters?
16. How many people and % have been trained in the importance and awareness of basic Business Improvement issues?
17. How many people and % have been trained in Business Improvement and to what level?
18. What savings were generated last year through Business Improvement?
19. How do managers motivate people to engage in Business Improvement?
20. What % of time do people spend on Business Improvement?
21. How are projects/improvements communicated so that others can learn from them and implement them in their area?

22. How many quality communications have there been from senior managers on the topic of BI in the last year?
23. How many times in the last year has there been a communication about a success in the field of Business Improvement?
24. Do all roles and responsibilities or job descriptions in the business mention that Business Improvement is an essential part of their role?
25. Is there a system or process for capturing savings and improvements in the business?

Conducting this short diagnostic on your business will start the process of speaking with data; it will give you an idea of where you are and what is possible. The diagnostic should take the approach of interviews, discussions with relevant personnel, desk research and questionnaires as a minimum. We would recommend that you review your findings with your deployment champion so you can start to assess and understand the size of your deployment challenge.

We would also suggest that you review and develop a list of potential risks and barriers to the implementation of a Business Improvement culture into your organisation. Some typical lists that need to be overcome are shown below. This is by no means an exhaustive list but will give you an idea of areas to investigate. It may be that using a Stakeholder analysis would also be beneficial at this stage. That way, you can gauge the impact and level of support for different people or stakeholder groups.

Possible barriers or risks:

- The senior management team does not have a common understanding of what is possible, where they are or what can be achieved.
- Some senior managers are not open-minded about change.

- Some senior managers are nervous about their capability to change.
- Senior management does not have enough time to plan and implement the change so they abdicate responsibility further down the organisation.
- The organisation does not know where to start or how to plan the change.
- There is union opposition due to a lack of communication or understanding.
- Middle managers do not want to change because they fear a loss of power and influence.
- Lower-level staff are resistant to change because they see no 'benefit' to them in doing so.
- Internal systems make it too complicated to change.
- Legislation stops change from happening because it 'must be done this way'.
- There is insufficient time available to train people or run projects.
- There is insufficient money available to invest in the infrastructure, processes and systems required to make this a success.
- HR does not want to change their processes, way of working and looking at the world.
- Line managers are not motivated or keen on changing the way they work.
- Everyone wants and expects results too quickly.
- There is no internal mechanism to monitor and control projects and activities.
- The lack of accurate business data slows down the progress.
- There is a general lack of appetite in the business for change.

These risks and barriers are very common in many organisations but by listing them and understanding where resistance may come from, you can start to plan your sense of urgency, your need for change and build your case for change.

Your case for change will typically have to be presented to the senior executives in your business. You will need to communicate the results of your diagnostic of where you are today. You may have to include some form of marketing analysis including competitor analysis, PESTLE analysis, etc. Lastly, you will have to show the risks and barriers to implementation. Presenting this case for change however will only be successful if your senior executives:

1. Understand business improvement and why it is essential.
2. Accept the results of your diagnostic and your current situation. Happy talk at senior levels, head in the sand and nonacceptance that there is a problem typically means that the business will not move forward.

Education of the executives can be done through running champion training to bring them up to a common understanding of Business Improvement and Lean Six Sigma. However, be aware that many will not engage, think they already know it all and are resistant to change. Anyone looking to implement Business Improvement must start to engage in a change management strategy to influence their executive team even before they get a chance to pitch the idea of deploying Business Improvement. This is a whole area that you will have to develop and understand.

If we can gain acceptance of our sense of urgency and build or case for change, then we can move to stage 2 of the model.

Step 2 Create a vision for the future and prepare for the journey

Imagine a company where external customers are delighted on a daily basis, where you outperform your competitors by a large margin, and staff are always looking to find new ways to make your customer's experience even better. Imagine a business where the internal customers are actually identified, they get what they want when they want it and in the way that they want it. They are constantly asked by those that supply them how we can make your life easier or better. Regulators are so delighted with how you treat them that they hold you up as a shining example of what others should do. Imagine a company where the staff actively look for, identify and solve customer and business issues on a daily basis, in a company where they are happy, work in teams and understand the importance of outstanding customer service.

Imagine a company where they work with their suppliers to identify ways to make their end customers happier. A company where they don't have any processes which only 1 or 2 people can deliver, where they have standard ways of running processes based on best practice and everyone adheres to them. A place where they constantly identify non-value added wasteful steps and remove them so that the business becomes more profitable and effective. Imagine a business that has education, training and personal development of its staff as a central goal.

To us, that sounds like a great organisation, with innovation and customer service as core goals. However, the first step on a journey to Business Improvement deployment is to identify your own end-goal. It is important to be as specific as possible and to communicate this throughout the entire organisation, so that everyone is pulling in the same direction. Business Improvement deployments are only truly successful if full buy-in is achieved across the company, at every level.

Engaging everyone at the outset

Total engagement is necessary for improvements to be as effective as possible, but how do you change the existing culture within an organisation? The key lies in clear communication, continued support and leading by example. Unsurprisingly, therefore, the buy-in of senior management is absolutely vital.

Unfortunately, this essential step is often overlooked. Our research suggests that over 60% of businesses are using Business Improvement methodologies. However, of these, 50% said that very few people within the organisation know about Lean Six Sigma and a further 25% said only one or two people were aware of the methodology.

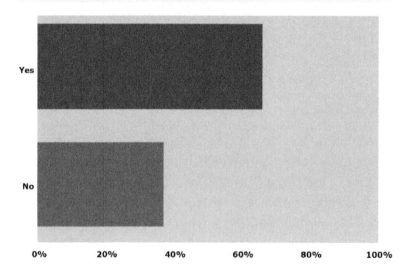

DO YOU CURRENTLY USE LEAN SIX SIGMA OR BUSINESS IMPROVEMENT PROCESSES?

HOW WOULD YOU DESCRIBE THE CURRENT LEVEL OF KNOWLEDGE OF LEAN SIX SIGMA IN YOUR ORGANISATION?

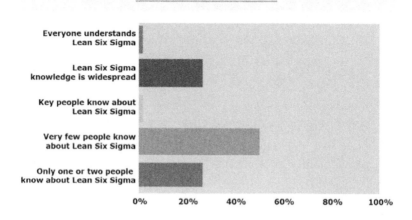

Business Improvement such as Lean Six Sigma is not a magic bullet, so senior managers must be aware that improvements will not happen overnight, and ensure that expectations are carefully managed throughout the company. Structurally, the company must make changes so that the strategic business goals are aligned with the Business Improvement goals, and ensure this change in focus becomes the new normal.

In practice this means appraisals and KPIs will need to be adapted to drive the correct behaviour; the benefits of the change must be clearly and effectively communicated in a way that highlights the relevance to employees; and there must be a defined process established for collecting, monitoring and solving the problems raised across the business.

Senior managers can start to influence behaviours very quickly by subtly changing how they act and talk about the business.

Senior management knowledge and commitment

Senior managers must lead by example and drive the change through the business. The first thing they need to realise is that this is not something that will happen overnight. They must plan for at least a year about how they will design, run and control the change as well as how they will monitor improvements. Without their commitment and energy, the cultural change will be far more difficult. They need to have a common understanding of what they are signing up to and then put in place a plan to make it happen. This plan might not be made visible but requires time and effort to put in place.

- Start asking people for data
- Set rules and stick to them
- Don't demand solutions without data
- Ask people to quantify the cost of a problem
- Ask people to share their ideas for standardisation
- Spend time talking about quality, customer service and business improvement and reiterate the importance of them at every opportunity
- Put Business Improvement on the monthly agenda at the board meeting
- If there is any Business Improvement activity in the company, show a genuine interest
- Communicate any Business Improvement activity in the company
- Start every meeting, workshop or chat with updates or thoughts on Business Improvement

As the saying goes, failing to prepare is preparing to fail. Organisations often launch a Business Improvement programme without developing a clear and coherent vision of what the future needs to look like. It is only when a company vision that everyone can work towards has been created and properly communicated that it can begin in earnest.

As such, the senior executive or steering committee working with a deployment champion must develop not only the sense of urgency but the vision for the future and the plan to get there.

Step Three: Establish the structure for success

Core to the success of Business Improvement is training and education. Without the correct tools, employees will be unable to effectively identify problems, make changes and track progress.

However, the degree of training required will vary depending on your starting point and your end-goals. Lean Six Sigma is one of the most widely used and well-known Business Improvement methodologies, and the approach we recommend. There are a number of key roles within every Lean Six Sigma deployment and these are:

The **Sponsor** or **Champion** are the people who are paving the way for the project, ensuring efforts are focused in the right area and that resources are made available.

Black Belts run large-scale complex projects and manage teams of people, so they need to have a robust technical understanding of Lean Six Sigma and the softer communication and influencing skills.

Green Belts run smaller, more departmentally-focused projects and often work on larger scale projects under the instruction of Black Belts. They need a good technical understanding and must have the soft skills required to work closely with people at all levels.

Yellow Belts may help out on smaller projects, but this level of training is usually given to anyone who could benefit from an awareness of Business Improvement in their daily role.

We recommend that all staff have training in the basics of Business Improvement such as waste and variation; that middle managers are given a clear understanding of the goals of Business Improvement and reassured about its purpose, and that senior managers have an awareness of the concepts to help with strategic planning and deployment.

Developing the deployment plan

Once they have been trained in the key concepts, senior managers must spend time developing a plan for the steps needed to deploy the change in the business, starting with how they will cascade the goals/KPIs of the business. How will they reward success? How will they engage staff and in what order? What will they do if people don't engage?

Leadership changes

The leader's role and attitudes need to change. They need to walk the talk and lead by example. They need to put customers internal and external first and act in the right way. They need to spend time working on improvement projects, motivating others who are engaged in Business Improvement, monitoring performance and working on strategy rather than tactical operation elements. They need to consider how this will be done; how time will be freed up, etc.

Cultural changes

The culture needs to be one where people are happy and encouraged to identify and solve problems. It needs to be one where blame is not the first or last step when something goes wrong. We need a culture where we speak with data and share information. We need a culture where working in teams is encouraged and where people share information and skills so that black arts are removed. What needs to be adapted?

Reward and recognition

Reward and recognition systems would need to encourage customer service improvement and business improvement. This means implementing new KPIs, which drive more than just functional excellence in a chosen role.

Systems

Systems will need to be in place which make it easy to track projects, monitor who has engaged, how large the benefits have been, where the issues are that need to be addressed, which processes are effective and those that are not. Systems need to make it easy to identify issues as items such as complaints, website activity, employee identified issues, feedback forms, surveys, focus groups, etc. All data needs to be joined up.

Processes & procedures

Standard processes need to be in place for every aspect of the business. 'Black arts' and variations need to be eradicated so that the business can always deliver what the customer requires, every time. Processes will be put in place to validate issues, prioritise problems and assign them to members of the team who will have the capacity and skills to solve them.

Team working

Team working is essential to obtain the real root cause of a problem, develop the best solution and implement the solution quickly and permanently.

The role of management

Managers will be motivators, communicators and coaches to their teams. They will always communicate through data so that issues can be resolved rather than hidden. Managers will work as un-blockers if problems arise and support people as they challenge and develop the business.

KPIs

Managers will be measured on how many ideas their people have generated and how many were implemented. They will be asked to prove how they have improved customer service and the business. Their secondary measure will be how well their function performed.

All staff will be asked to identify and solve issues and the business will be proud to share the issues it has solved and how it did so.

Work climate and motivation

The working environment will be enjoyable. People will be given time to identify and solve problems. Blame will not occur and honest feedback will always be given to help individuals grow, customer service to improve and business performance to flourish. People will motivate and drive each other to identify and solve issues. Healthy competition will develop between functions and processes.

Logistics for the deployment

All aspects of the deployment need to be outlined as planned so that when the vision is shared, you have answers to all the inevitable questions which will be raised, such as:

- How will delegates be selected for training?
- How will projects be selected?
- What level of training will be started?
- Who will deliver the training?
- Who will coach delegates?
- How will we certify delegates?
- How will progress of projects be monitored and reported?
- How will we keep track of and sign off benefits?
- How will we share best practices and lessons learned?
- Which software will we use for Statical analysis?
- Which subjects will be delivered during the training?
- What additional support will we provide delegates?

- What other training can we offer other than traditional Lean Six Sigma training?
- How will we engage and train others such as Yellow Belts, sponsors, etc?
- How will we reward success?
- How will we communicate our plan and obtain feedback?

Governance and control

A Steering Committee is going to be required to keep everything in check and visibly demonstrate focus within the organisation.

The Steering Committee structure could be as follows:

- Who – senior leadership team
- Meeting frequency – monthly
- Time – 1 hour per month at board meeting
- Purpose – drive, monitor and motivate continuous improvement in the business
- Facilitator – the deployment champion
- Agenda items
    - Monthly progress
    - Year to date benefits
    - Project selection
    - Issues
    - Presentations from Green Belts or others (10mins)

Senior Managers will need to understand who the supporters, advocates and potential blockers to their cultural change are. They will then need to develop a strategy for different functions, individuals and processes.

It is best to start in one process or one area of the business. Pick or ask for volunteers (identify people you want and make them want to be on the training). Make it something people want to be curious enough to ask about. Don't call it an initiative or a program or a new way of working. Just start talking about it. Put up a website where you can share what is happening – training, project success, and certification – just start it without any ceremony. People will want to engage.

Every improvement in the company can be driven through the governance of the Steering Committee; this way, only prioritised important activities are worked on and monitored in the business. This stops individuals from working on what they think is important or what they want to work on, which of course can be a waste of time and focus.

Communications

Communicate, communicate, communicate – that is one of the key secrets to successful deployment of Lean Six Sigma or Business Improvement. Right from the moment we start a program, we must explain why, how, when, your involvement and sell the vision we have developed. It cannot be overstated how important communications are to the success of Business Improvement.

If possible, make this a role in your deployment and try as many different channels to communicate and methods and don't forget to get feedback constantly. If you do, you can get more and more people on your side and start to influence and engage everyone from day 1.

Step Four: Run improvement projects

The organisation must set up how it will run and control projects, activities and improvements. Each type of activity will have slightly different approaches but the overall governance should be the same.

Once all the processes are in place, the only thing left to do is to start running projects. But first, you need to generate ideas. What are the problems? What are the priorities? What would see the biggest impact on customer service?

It's often simple to identify the first batch of problems, but for a business to continuously improve, there needs to be a regular flow of issues that can be categorised, prioritised and dealt with accordingly. The systems put in place during the deployment stage will be an integral part of this process as they will deliver a constant flow of data, trends, demands and issues.

Further ideas will come from the regular reviews by the Steering Committee, customer feedback and working closely with suppliers. Suppliers and customers provide a huge resource of opportunities, so their views should be captured and closely reviewed.

Problems can be broken down into three main types of improvement projects:

Quick win projects

These will be ideas-generated in a local area or function that can be implemented without any other outside assistance. They will make a quick impact, are low risk, low cost and within the control of one manager. They do not require detailed data collection or root cause analysis. An example might be to paint a machine or to put in place a shadow board, or answer a particular customer issue.

DMAIC improvement projects

An improvement/issues hub should be created which captures all the areas to be worked on. They will come from a range of sources. After filtering, they will be allocated as a DMAIC project and an appropriately trained person will be tasked with solving the issue. Typically, these kinds of projects will require some analysis and investigation. The root causes are not known and neither is the solution. If they are, then they will be implemented as normal implementation projects. These are problems that need data to validate them and time spent to resolve them. An example might be to reduce the time it takes to complete a task.

Kaizen events

These problem areas have the same selection characteristics as a DMAIC project, however, some projects require resolution quicker than others. A Kaizen event would be run when there is a need for quick solutions or when there is an opportunity to utilise people who are on-site or can only be released for a short period of time.

Throughout the projects, the most important tool is data. So, it is essential that progress is meticulously tracked and that this is communicated. If it is impossible to prove the impact a project has had, it is much easier to slip back into bad habits.

	Quick Win Projects	DMAIC Improvement Projects	Kaizen Events
Purpose	To implement simple ideas or changes quickly	To solve complex issues permanently using a structured problem- solving process	Solve issues permanently and quickly.
Run by	The local area team	Trained Lean Six Sigma personnel – Yellow, Green or Black Belts	Trained Lean Six Sigma personnel – Yellow, Green or Black Belts
KPIs	How many ideas raised and by whom. How many ideas closed. The benefits of each idea. How many ideas have been rolled out to other areas of the business.	Number of projects completed. Number of projects to achieve their SMART goals. Running total of benefits achieved in this way.	Number of projects completed. Number of projects to achieve SMART goals. Running total of benefits achieved in this way. How many ideas have been rolled out to other areas of the business. Number of projects completed in the allocated time frame.
Controlled by	Area team leader, manager, supervisor.	Steering Committee, sponsors and champion.	Steering Committee, sponsors and champion.

Mechanism	Charts, spread sheets, or simple websites to consistently track and update	An improvement/ issues hub should be created which captures all the areas to be worked on from a number of sources. After filtering they will be allocated as a DMAIC project	These problems have the same selection characteristics as a DMAIC project, and Kaizen event would be run when there is a need for quick solutions
Process	Idea is raised by individual, customer, supplier or audit of the area. Weekly team leader gathers appropriate people for meeting and each idea is reviewed and classified as: Rejected – with feedback provided as to why. More information required – team leader needs more information from the person who raised the idea.	Ideas, issues or opportunities are entered into the ideas hub. Deployment Champion or Master Black Belt filters the ideas. The originator of the idea or issue is kept up to date with progress. Steering Committee discusses and prioritises the issues with the help of the prioritising tools and the Deployment Champion. Assign a sponsor and belt to complete the project.	Ideas, issues or opportunities are entered into the ideas hub. Deployment Champion or Master Black Belt filters the ideas. The originator of the idea or issue is kept up to date with progress. Steering Committee discusses and prioritises the issues. Assign a sponsor and belt to complete a Kaizen event. The Deployment Champion or Master Black Belt assigns the project to the Yellow, Green or Black Belt.
Process (cont'd)	Obtain data – team leader will collect some data to review the idea. Implement –implement the idea and collect data on the improvement so that it can be reported. Escalate idea to BI board – if the idea is seen as needing more resource, time or analysis the idea will be put into the ideas hub and reviewed as below.	The Deployment Champion or Master Black Belt completes 75% of the project charter and assigns the project to the Yellow, Green or Black Belt. Belt runs the project until completion. Completed ideas summarised for the monthly KPI.	Belt then runs a Kaizen event in the traditional manner. After the event, the Kaizen has 30 days to complete the actions and close off the project. Completed ideas summarised for the monthly KPI.
Review completed ideas and pass on those with scope elsewhere in the business			
Potential Issues	Ensure that ideas are not at odds with other projects, will fix the issue and progress is accurately reported.	Ensure that the scope of the project is not too large. Ensure feedback to person who raised the issue. Ensure that data is accurately collected. Don't rush the project to solutions.	Ensure that the scope of the project is not too large. Ensure feedback to person who raised the issue. Ensure that data is accurately collected. Ensure the actions are completed in 30 days.

Step Five: Rigorously track and communicate progress

The importance of monitoring and tracking cannot be overstated. Regular reviewing of projects serves several purposes – to illustrate to all employees it is a business priority, to ensure all projects are carried through to completion, and to measure the success of a Business Improvement implementation.

Without this tracking, it is easy for day-to-day tasks to take precedence and progress on improvement to be side-lined or abandoned. To be successful, it must become a priority. At every stage of the process, tracking should be in-built; it is a function of the Steering Committee, of the Business Improvement Champion and should be reflected in the KPIs of all relevant staff members.

To prevent focus on Business Improvement slipping, each person should ideally have at least one KPI related to Business Improvement. This makes continuous improvement the responsibility of everyone as part of their specific role, rather than resting accountability on a few key people's shoulders. We suggest managers have a broader range of KPIs linked to Business Improvement as they will act as a driving force within the company and that the organisation has strategic goals with associated KPIs.

Individual KPIs

- Number of ideas, issues and opportunities raised in the year
- Benefits generated by their ideas or solutions in the year
- Number of ideas implemented or teams involved in Manager KPIs
- Percentage of their direct reports who have engaged in business improvements
- Number of ideas generated in their area
- Number of projects run in their area
- Benefits generated in their area as a result of successful projects

Company KPIs

- Benefits of BI in the business
- Percentage of people who have engaged in BI
- Number of Kaizen, DMAIC projects, quick wins implemented
- Improvement in customer service
- Number of suppliers who have contributed to Business Improvement

Make progress visible

Communication of success, actions and activities of any change is vital to keep up momentum. As such, the importance of an effective communications plan and internal PR should not be overlooked. The deployment champion and the Steering Committee should take every chance to promote the new behaviours and attitudes that they expect from the business. They should reinforce anyone who has been engaged or shown imitative.

It's an unfortunate truth that the vast majority of Business Improvement project reports undersell and underwhelm when you first read them. Although the bones of the project may not be bad, a failure to present the results in an exciting and informative manner means that the true benefits of the project are buried in hard to read documents. The result is that the person or team responsible fails to get the recognition that they deserve, and that others in the business don't instantly see the benefit of Business Improvement.

In some cases, this can translate to a slowdown, or even bring a complete halt, to engagement throughout the company.

It usually takes a lot of effort for a company to undertake any form of Business Improvement. Normally, a champion pushes the cause and they eventually get signed off, sometimes reluctantly. But we know that for a company to whole-heartedly engage in Business Improvement, it needs the senior managers to understand and buy into the concept. They must be won over, they must be convinced, they must be persuaded.

The first pioneers who run the first projects are therefore crucial ambassadors for the change. They must be seen to have followed the structure and obtained good results. If they don't, it pushes the neutrals into negative territory and provides the initial naysayers with ammunition. The same shift in attitude can be seen when the first projects are delayed or take much longer than expected.

To avoid this, we think it is essential that the pioneers excel at promoting the successes, approach and benefits of Business Improvement. Getting off on an optimistic footing will give senior managers the confidence they need, and positivity will filter down in the organisation as people see and hear about the benefits. A very strong start neutralises the argument of the cynics.

Against this backdrop, why aren't the vast majority of projects I review great at selling the benefits? Why do they bury the improvements and fail to champion the cause? Why do so many people underplay their project successes and keep the information to themselves?

There are a variety of reasons:

- Our British culture – It's not in our nature to promote ourselves or our achievements for fear of being seen as arrogant or self-serving.
- Lack of skills – We don't know how to structure our projects and outcomes to maximise publicity internally.
- Lack of awareness – We don't realise ourselves what impact the changes will have.
- Lack of data – We have not collected the figures to show the cost savings, income generation or other benefits associated with our project so can't prove it.
- Lack of confidence – If we feel we could have achieved a better outcome with more time and resources, we feel embarrassed, regardless of the successes we have achieved.

So, what's the advice for people about to embark on their first project? How can they enhance their own reputation in the firm, their team's reputation and the reputation of the Business Improvement approach?

Recognise what you have achieved. Lots of projects don't realise what they have done. They don't look at the bigger picture and how this fits in. They don't spend enough time thinking about hard and soft benefits and the impact the solution has had on the business

Ensure that your problem statement or definition makes it clear how bad things were. Make it clear to anyone who reads it the terrible situation that was in existence. Don't sugar-coat it; tell it exactly as it is. If you have written a good problem statement, any stakeholder who reads it should be thinking that action needs taking immediately.

Make sure you show how the project relates to the corporate goals or the strategy of the business. If you do, then every senior manager in the place will be interested.

Make sure that through a stakeholder analysis you have understood which one of the senior managers solving this problem will help and then communicate this to them. Show them how this will help them achieve their goals or improve their performance.

Make sure you have the data to show the whole story. Your data collection plan needs to include all the key data for you to show the benefits and the size of the problem. Think about the questions you will be asked after the project – such as the impact on cost and resources – and collect the data now so you are able to make the comparison.

Ensure the final presentation tells a story. Use the data to make it rich and engaging. Structure the presentation to capture your audience and then slam home the benefits, both hard and soft. Use quotes from team members and other managers to give the story colour and life. Make it so that nobody can leave the room without understanding what the problem was, how you and your team solved it and the amazing benefits as a result.

Look for other areas in the company where you can roll out your solutions as this will amplify the benefits to the company and the positive press.

Ask to present it to other areas of the company. If you have a good story to tell, make sure you get maximum exposure – don't hide under a bushel.

If you have a communications team, talk to them about how you can get into the internal newsletter or share the story. They are always looking for material and will also help you shape the story most effectively.

Look to write a case study that you can use externally; this will help promote both the company and your team's success.

If you can correctly promote the project you have just completed, it has a massive effect on everyone – yourself, your team, your sponsor and business development in the business. It will maintain the momentum of Business Improvement and convince others to engage in the process.

It is essential that at every point in the deployment we communicate and engage it to make success happen.

3.6 Summary

To successfully deploy Lean Six Sigma into any company, you will need to treat this as a major change program. Select your change agents and follow the model above and you will have a greater chance of success. Make sure that you reflect on each part of the model. Communicate, Communicate, Communicate. Ensure that you convince everyone in the business why change is essential, why we must implement Lean Six Sigma. They should be able to explain to you why we must change the sense of urgency. If they can, you know they understand and we have a greater chance of success.

Involve as many people as possible in the design of your deployment. Paint and communicate in as many different ways what the future will look like and how you plan to get there. Train people in the correct way, with the right tools and make sure there is something in it for them when they finish their training.

Plan your deployment, think about the infrastructure needed and answer people's questions. Make sure you can show that you have thought it through, how it will work, what it means to them and how it will impact them. Pick the right people to be your pioneers or change agents, give them time to solve your first projects and make sure those projects are selected properly. Ensure that the projects will provide strategic benefit and when they are complete, shout about it from the rooftops.

Keep people engaged and communicate what is happening and collect feedback. As you progress, track what is happening, particularly benefits, and make Business Improvement a key aspect of all meetings and discussions.

Over time, you will see your culture change. Business Improvement will become a way of life. Problems will be solved that you didn't even know about; all you will see is an improvement in profits, customer service and staff satisfaction. Keep the faith and keep pushing through and this can be a reality in any business.

Section 4

How to train, motivate and educate your people

4.1 What are the essential roles in Lean Six Sigma?

In order to deploy Lean Six Sigma successfully, you need to understand the required roles for success. Once you understand the definitions of these roles, you can review your own situation and adapt them to suit your exact needs. Outlined below are the roles that are typically seen in companies who successfully deploy Lean Six Sigma. This does not mean that you have to have one or more people in each role. It doesn't mean you need the numbers mentioned; we only discuss them in this section so you have the knowledge to make your own decisions.

Lean Six Sigma has evolved a jargon of its own, with different coloured Belts and specialist roles. This might seem confusing at first but it clearly sets out what each person involved is expected to do and it provides a standard so that no matter where you are in the world, when you say you are a Green Belt or a Sponsor, they are understood.

Let's start by looking at the structure you would typically see in a mature Lean Six Sigma organisation.

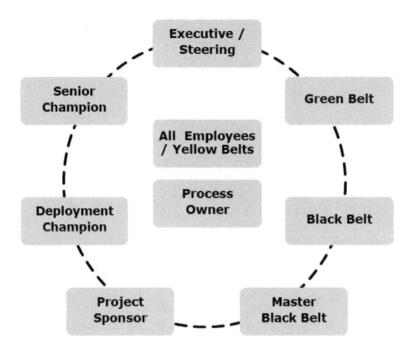

This diagram shows a lot of different roles you would see in a mature and possibly large organisation. In a smaller organisation, roles may be combined and performed by one person. However, defining the roles as separate in this way helps to clarify the different responsibilities for each.

There are two kinds of activities associated with a Lean Six Sigma programme: those involved with one project and those involved with several at a deployment level. All the roles have some responsibilities in both activities but let's start with those roles mainly involved in the deployment, organising Lean Six Sigma and leading Lean Six Sigma. We will then look at the roles associated with solving problems and running projects.

The steering or executive committee or executive leadership

We will start with one of the most critical roles; the executive leadership. Not every company has a steering committee overseeing their Lean Six Sigma activities, but the data clearly shows that companies who use this to drive the use of Lean Six Sigma from the top get more success from their Business Improvement programmes than those which don't.

The steering or executive committee is the driving force behind the Lean Six Sigma deployment. It is usually formed from a group of very Senior Managers, Directors, or Vice Presidents of the company. They are not experts in Lean Six Sigma, but they all understand it and see it as the way to get improvements done in the business.

They meet on a regular basis – normally around once per month – to discuss the deployment, review the status and plan the future. At the steering committee meeting, they would typically review the benefits already secured and those identified in the future for the whole program. They would review the status of the projects which are underway at a high level, by counting how many projects are in each of the DMAIC stages. This allows them to predict when further benefits will be delivered to their organisation.

They would also look at the resources they have, i.e. the Green and Black Belts, and select the next projects they have to work on. Remember, if an organisation has been set up correctly, then they will use their Green and Black Belts to transform their business and solve major business issues. It is therefore important that the steering committee pick the projects that the Green and Black Belts work on.

At each monthly meeting, the steering committee may have some Green and Black Belts present their projects to them. As well as informing the senior leadership, this is a major opportunity for the Green or Black Belt to gain visibility and recognition.

The steering committee has developed the vision for Lean Six Sigma and is accountable on behalf of the organisation to make the change happen, and then delegate the responsibility to achieve that to the

Deployment and Senior Champions. So, they will ask the Deployment Champion or the Senior Champion to give them progress reports on what is going well, what needs their attention and what is not going so well so they can get involved as required.

The role of the Executive Leadership is to:

- Make the decision to implement the Lean Six Sigma initiative
- Develop accountability
- Set meaningful goals and objectives for the corporation
- Set performance expectations for the corporation
- Ensure continuous improvement in the process
- Eliminate barriers

The Deployment Champions and Senior Champions

The Senior and Deployment Champions can make or break a Lean Six Sigma deployment and it's important to put people in the role who believe in it and can communicate their passion to others. They manage the delivery of benefits and create a Lean Six Sigma culture in their business.

Champions should be:

- Accountable for creating a Lean Six Sigma culture in their organisation
- Must know the methodology and use it
- It helps if they are certified to at least Green Belt level so they understand how projects are run
- They should participate in networks outside their specific business

The Senior and Deployment Champions' job is to listen to the steering or executive leadership and get the Lean Six Sigma improvement programme running. They decide how to achieve, implement and monitor the success of the company's Business

Improvement objectives. They may have a responsibility for the whole company, a single function or a single geographic location.

The Champions identify people with the right skills to be assigned to Lean Six Sigma roles, organise training, select projects, track progress and report benefits to the steering committee.

They also act as line managers for Master Black Belts and some Black Belts if they are part of the company's central Continuous Improvement group. The Champions don't get involved in the day-to-day oversight of each project unless one gets into trouble. But they are often expected to ensure that the company gets the most value from its Lean Six Sigma programme.

The Champions are the visible leaders of a Lean Six Sigma deployment, so are looked to for recognition and reward. One role of a Senior Champion is to present certificates to successful Black Belts.

The Champion or Champions act as a Programme Management Office for a Lean Six Sigma deployment. They should track the success of the deployment by measuring benefits, confirming that trained Belts have completed projects and making sure the pipeline of projects stays healthy.

The Senior Champion sometimes acts as secretary to the steering committee and works closely with them to make sure projects are chosen that are in line with the company's strategic goals. A Champion may be a full-time role in a large organisation or at the start of a big deployment, but it is common for the Champions to fulfil their responsibilities alongside another role.

Master Black Belt (MBB)

A Master Black Belt, or MBB, is a full-time Continuous Improvement job. They normally report to a senior person in the organisation and work across the organisation at all levels.

Many companies don't have a person with this experience at the start of their Lean Six Sigma deployment. Consultants, including 100% Effective, can perform this role until a company develops the capability to train and coach Green and Black Belts themselves.

Responsibilities include:

- Providing advice and counsel to Executive Staff
- Providing training and support
- In-class training
- One-to-one coaching
- Developing sustainability for the business
- Facilitating cultural change

Now, we'll look at those roles mainly involved in the delivery of single Lean Six Sigma projects.

Project Sponsor

The first critical role in every project is the Project Sponsor, sometimes referred to as the Project Champion.

Every project should have a Project Sponsor or Project Champion. This is the person who wants the problem to be solved; they don't have the Lean Six Sigma skills to solve the problem by themselves, so the role of the Green or Black Belt is to help them solve the problem using the DMAIC approach. As it is the Sponsor's problem, it is also their responsibility to make sure it is solved. That responsibility starts by defining the goals and scope of the project.

The Sponsor must be there to help the Green or Black Belt if there are any problems or barriers which they are unable to overcome alone. Normally, the Green or Black Belt will go to the Sponsor if there are issues such as not getting time or commitment from people, if a manager is not being cooperative or if there is an issue which is higher up in the organisation than they can deal with. In these instances, the Sponsor takes the role of sorting this out – after all, it is their problem they are trying to solve, so it is in their interest to help.

The Sponsor also makes sure the project remains relevant. They need to keep the Green or Black Belt informed of changes in the external environment that could affect the project. If they fail to do this, the project may do a great job but solve a problem that no longer needs fixing.

As part of their responsibilities, the Sponsor leads each Gate Review with the Green or Black Belt. This happens at the end of each DMAIC phase and is where the Green or Black Belt reports progress on the project and gets approval to move from one phase to another.

Most Sponsors need to plan around 1 to 3 hours for dealing with the project and their Green or Black Belt. If they are getting an important project completed, then this is time well spent and they should be willing to spend it with their Green or Black Belt. If they are not willing to spend this time, then it suggests that the project or problem is not that important to them – either the project is a bad choice, or (as sometimes happens when a Sponsor is assigned to a project by other people), a different Sponsor is needed.

Here are some of the main responsibilities of the Project Sponsor:

- Defines project scope and goals
- Obtains necessary project resources and eliminates   roadblocks
- Keeps the project aware of external changes
- Leads each DMAIC Gate Review
- Needs to be available for one to three hours per week

If a Sponsor is active, understands their role and takes the time to support the Green or Black Belt then a project has a very good chance of success. Unfortunately, this is not always the case as Sponsors are often given the role without realising what it means, thinking that it is the Green or Black Belt's responsibility to do everything and spend no time helping out.

To get around this, successful organisations provide Project Sponsor training. This is typically a 1-day session where Sponsors are trained in what Lean Six Sigma is, what a Sponsor is, and their role and responsibilities. They are not taught all the Lean Six Sigma tools and techniques but are taught what type of questions to ask Green and Black Belts during Gate Reviews. This means that the Sponsor can sound credible and ensure that their problems are solved correctly using the DMAIC and Lean Six Sigma principles.

Sponsor training is often missed out though, as these people are usually very busy already, and will say they don't have time to attend. However, those who do attend the training always see the benefits, both to them as an individual, and to the organisation as a whole. The Sponsor after all is an integral – and critical – part of the Lean Six Sigma process. And if the project is really going to solve their problem for them, they should be willing to invest the time learning how to give that project the greatest chance of success.

Black Belts (BBs)

Lean Six Sigma projects are delivered by teams led by a Green or Black Belt. Although some Black Belts and Green Belts don't run any projects but just do the training so that they can use the methodology to solve problems robustly, this is the exception rather than the rule.

Black Belts typically spend all their time running projects and may be asked to run two or three projects simultaneously. Their projects are normally complex strategic or cross-functional projects, whereas the Green Belt will only spend a fraction of their time working on projects and these are more limited in scope.

Black Belts have attended a 12 to 15-day training course and to certify, will have gained experience by completing a number of projects. They are often seen as change agents in the organisation, for which they need a variety of attributes that we will talk about later.

Responsibilities include:

- Serving as a Project team leader
- Facilitating DMAIC teams in applying Lean Six Sigma methods to solve problems
- Working cross-functionally
- Contributing to the accomplishment of organisational goals
- Providing technical support to improvement efforts

Green Belts (GBs)

Let's take a look at what the Green Belt does. A Green Belt's role is a part-time assignment and the Green Belt does this as well as their day-to-day job. Green Belts can either run projects with a limited scope on their own, or they can run part of bigger projects with support from a Black Belt. A Green Belt will usually work on a project in their own functional area, while a Black Belt may be asked to work in a function that they know little about.

Reflecting the different time commitments of each belt, Green Belt projects need to be quick and easy to implement so should take a matter of weeks from start to finish, whereas Black Belt projects may take many months. Green Belts are trained through a 5 or 6-day training program and learn all the key skills they will need. If they have further issues, then they will go to a Black or Master Black Belt for support.

Green Belts are the main Business Improvement resource of most companies deploying Lean Six Sigma as they get through lots of projects and therefore deliver benefits quickly.

Responsibilities include:

- Leading projects, usually in their own functional area
- Being involved in identifying improvement opportunities

- Being involved in continuous improvement efforts
- Applying basic tools
- Creating Process Control Systems
- Supporting projects with process knowledge and data collection

All employee's involvement - Yellow Belts (YBs)

Yellow Belt training or awareness training is often given to all intended members of the Lean Six Sigma project teams. This is done as both a communications exercise so that people know what is going on and why, but also so that when a Green or Black Belt asks them to join their team, they are not having to educate them from scratch. Sometimes, Yellow Belts are asked to lead short rapid-improvement projects with a specific goal that has been defined by a Black Belt.

Yellow Belt training is typically 1 or 2 days and covers what Lean Six Sigma is, why it is done, and how to do it with an overview of each stage and some of the key tools.

Process Owners

The next role is that of the Process Owner. The Process Owner is the person who has overall responsibility for the process being improved and will have the authority to make changes to the process. They will also be the person who takes ownership for the process improvements once the project is complete, therefore it is vital that they are involved and supportive of all project activities, even if they don't have the time to be a core member of the project team.

If the process being improved spans across several departments, which is common especially in a Black Belt project, the Process Owner will need to have authority to make changes across all of the departments. It is not recommended to have more than one Process Owner – our experience is that it often hinders the success of the project. In these situations, the single Process Owner must be identified before the project starts; don't start the project and hope it will sort itself out later because it probably won't, and the lack of clarity will slow up and possibly stop the project.

In some projects, the Process Owner may also be the Sponsor. This isn't necessary, although it does make them very supportive of the project and committed to implementing the improvements.

Sometimes, the Green Belt is the Owner of the Process (it is rare for this to be a problem in Black Belt projects). This situation is not impossible to handle but does require care. At the end of the project, the Green Belt must hand over responsibility for the improvements to the Process Owner. If these two roles are the same person, the Green Belt may cut corners in completing the Control Plan since they expect to carry on managing the process. However, if this person changes jobs a few months later, the new process is insufficiently documented or measured, and the benefits of the Lean Six Sigma project will be lost.

All these roles are needed in a complex and mature organisation for a successful deployment, but what about a smaller organisation or one which is just starting down the road of Lean Six Sigma?

What roles do I need in my organisation?

Although you might not have different people taking each role, somebody will still perform each of them. For example, one of the Directors who sits on the executive board was the person who wanted to start the Lean Six Sigma programme so she is the Senior Champion, and she is organising everything, so is also the Deployment Champion. She has chosen 6 Green Belts in her functional area and is the Sponsor for all of their projects as she is best placed to remove any obstacles they encounter. After she has run her pilot projects, she will roll out Lean Six Sigma to a wider group using Yellow Belt training.

Some companies don't have any Black Belts at first, and only train their staff to Green Belt level. They find they can get quick and significant returns by limiting their projects to Green Belt complexity; it's also quicker to get started as they don't need so much time away from their jobs to be trained and to deliver projects. Eventually, if bigger and more complex problems need to be solved, they identify a suitable Black Belt from one of their Green Belts and train them further.

Many companies don't have a full-time Master Black Belt, instead using outside MBBs to deliver their training and coaching.

So, although there are many different roles in a Lean Six Sigma programme, this doesn't mean a major increase in headcount. There are many different roles in order to bring clarity to what each one does; as we have shown you, many roles can be performed by a single person.

You must decide what works best for your organisation.

4.2 Skills of an effective Green or Black Belt

A future Green or Black Belt will need to use certain skills to be effective, regarding both Lean Six Sigma and in the workplace in general. Let's look at their roles and skills in more detail.

Whichever business function the Black Belt originally came from, they need to have some key attributes, skills and attitudes to be successful.

- Black Belts are Change Agents
- Challenge conventional wisdom by demonstrating the successful application of new methodologies
- Carry a very high level of peer respect and are clearly seen as leaders
- Effectively manage project and business risk
- Lead the way to breakthrough improvement

- Stimulate management thinking by posing new ways of doing things

Black Belts will become experts in the tools and techniques associated with Lean Six Sigma and will use their skills to solve strategic and high impact problems in the organisation. These problems have often been unsolved for a long time. As a result, Black Belts normally obtain a high profile and their general understanding of different areas within the organisation are often much broader than their peers.

This is great for the Black Belt, and it also explains why so many effective Black Belts get promoted as management recognise their skills.

There is however a potential downside to a Black Belt running successful projects and delivering great benefits. If not managed well, they may become frustrated if they see themselves doing great work and not being recognised. This is why, even at the start of a Lean Six Sigma deployment, it's necessary to think about how the Black Belt will be rewarded and recognised.

A Black Belt assignment is full time and usually lasts 2 or 3 years, at the end of which the certified Black Belt usually moves back into a day-to-day role, taking their Lean Six Sigma skills with them. If it is not clear what role they will move to, or if there are no positions available at the end of their assignment, they will become unsettled and look elsewhere for their next career challenge.

The skills of a highly effective Black Belt are very transferable and employers are eager for this kind of person to join their company. So, if not looked after, there is a risk that they will move on. A star performer could be lost, and the return on the time and effort invested in training them is less.

Some companies look at this problem and decide not to train Black

Belts because of the risk they will leave. This is a mistake, as it overlooks the massive benefits the Black Belt will deliver in just their first one or two projects. It is far better to train them, use them, and keep them. So, if you have a good Green or Black Belt, look after them.

TYPES OF BLACK BELTS

Technical skills (vertical axis)

Technical Experts
Understands technical details well, but is less comfortable working with others.

Effective BBs
Naturally skilled in technical and social areas, increased with practice through project delivery.

Showmen
Fantastic at working with people. Understands enough of the training to get results.

Social skills (horizontal axis)

There are different types of Black Belts and some are more effective than others in different situations. One way to look at the skills of different Black Belts is to compare their technical and change management skills.

The technical experts are people who understood all the training in real detail. They can get to grips with the statistical side from first principles, know all the formulas and can solve almost any problem you put in front of them. But they are less comfortable working with people or teams. You get the best out of these people by giving them things to do on their own.

Showmen are fantastic at working with people. They can convince them to do anything, they can sell to anyone, and they are great at presenting, facilitating and motivating. They get things done through the power of their personality or network. They have completed all the training and although they might not have totally absorbed it all, they've understood enough that they can get results.

Effective Black Belts are people who have both these skillsets so they can solve complex problems but also sell the benefits and influence others to accept the solutions. It is rare for us to find people with both of these skills sets naturally so we need to ensure that we develop our training and support to ensure that they can become skilled in both. If you don't, then you will need to ensure that the team working on a problem has these skillsets between them.

The more effective Black Belts are at assessing both areas of their development, the easier they will be able to develop the skills where they are weakest. This requires Black and Green Belts to have the personal awareness, which is of course a skill on its own. I recall coaching two Black Belts who were both managers in a business in the UK. Both were given the same training, the same opportunity for coaching and at the same time to deliver projects. Interestingly, one of the Black Belts always turned up for coaching sessions, completed activities and projects on time. They asked about their personal performance in all aspects of Lean Six Sigma and took feedback from everyone onboard. The other missed session after session because they were too busy in their opinion (both delegates had the same workload), they never asked for feedback and they just wanted to get their day job done. Over the years, the first Black Belt has continued to ask for feedback in each of the companies they have subsequently gone on to work in. Each move has seen them move up the corporate ladder and today they are the CEO of a major corporation in the UK. The other has advanced one or two levels but is still a manager in the same company.

When I analyse the difference, one thing stands out for me. The first Black Belt had loads of personal awareness. They wanted to improve and had the drive to do so. The other got so engrossed in the here and now that they couldn't see how to improve. We want our Black Belts to have loads of personal awareness and to understand that they can always improve and get better.

To be an effective Black Belt, you need to be competent in both social and technical skills. You also need to realise that you are in effect a change agent or catalyst for the business. You are not just a person who solves problems or analyses data; your role is so much more. Challenging the status quo is almost expected from a Black Belt; you don't just accept what you are told, you challenge it. This should mean you become a nuisance to management. No matter what they say without the data, they should be challenged, they should ask for proof, they should suggest other ways. They become a constant group of people who challenge the business and management to do better.

Black Belts will ask the awkward questions others think about. They do this as their confidence grows with each project they complete, every senior management meeting they attend and each success they have. Their training makes them confident, they only speak with data so people find it hard to challenge them. They make change happen.

Good potential Black Belts will have a lot of respect from their colleagues and are the type of people that others look up to, indicating that they have the necessary people skills to be effective.

Black Belts will run projects that make a substantial difference to a business or organisation. These projects carry risk: the risk of not doing them at all, of not doing them correctly, of a consequential impact on other parts of the business. So, we must select the right Black Belts in the first place as they will reduce risk on our business, make improvements and ensure that all areas of our company are protected from the impact of changes make in other areas. They can look for the unforeseen circumstances of change made in one part of the business impacting another.

Black Belts should always be looking to develop further, adapt their thinking and broaden their knowledge of tools and techniques. They should be constantly striving for new learning in all aspects of business, including people and processes. In effect, Black Belts should be the driving force in developing the business and should constantly bring new ideas to management.

When we have studied the Green and Black Belts who consistently get results, they behave in similar ways.

BEHAVIOURS OF AN EFFECTIVE BELT

Drive and enthusiasm.	Determination to do things right and see them to completion.
Ability to challenge the norm at any level in the organisation.	Great people skills and the ability to build rapport at any level.
Great networking skills inside and out of the business.	Disciplined to use the approach under severe pressure, to do things quicker and with less robustness.

Great Green and Black Belts have loads of enthusiasm. It is very important as people are far more likely to engage with people who have these qualities. Effective Belts also are very determined to get things done. They are dogged to follow a project all the way through, no matter what obstacles you put in their way.

Enthusiasm and drive are qualities you can't easily teach, so if you find Green or Black Belt candidates with these attributes, then you should put them through the training since the other skills are far easier to teach!

Effective Belts are happy to challenge the norm, no matter where it is or who states it. They distrust the status quo and are always looking to change things. They don't just accept what managers say if they think there is a better way to do things. This is important as you don't want the Belt to be put off at the first sign of resistance.

We also want our effective Green or Black Belt to be creative – in how they solve problems, how they get information and data and how they come up with solutions.

This generally means they have to be good at building relationships and rapport with all kinds of people. That helps when they need support and assistance, as does having the ability to network. If you are effective, you generally find you have the ability to network with people so that when you hit snags, you have a group of people you can call on from all walks of life to help you out.

They also need to have the discipline to follow the DMAIC process, no matter what. They need to follow the rules and not be swayed. When managers are forcing them for quick fixes, they need to say, 'no, we need to ensure we solve this problem once and for all, which means doing it right'.

This means they must be self-reliant, they must not have to ask for permission all the time or ask what to do next. They shouldn't need to be constantly shown how to do things but work it out for themselves. They are the kind of people who just get on with it, regardless of what obstacles are put in their way. So, they are self-starters who need little management.

They also constantly look to develop themselves and ask for feedback. Good Black Belts know that they must continue learning and developing; this expectation is one of the key differentiators between Green and Black Belts.

Not only do they need these attributes, but they need to have some specific skills. So what skills do you think the ideal Black or Green Belt has? See diagram.

Many of these skills are the typical skills needed to excel in any business situation. However, these basic skills have often not been taught or practised, so Belts may not be as good as they should be at them. The better you become at these basic skills, the better a Black or Green Belt you will become.

The key message here is that the technical tools associated with Lean Six Sigma are only one element. Most Green and Black Belt courses spend all their time teaching those technical tools because they assume everyone already has the other skills. Unfortunately, this isn't true: we often come across candidates who say they hate presenting or they don't understand change management, for example.

Very few Black or Green Belts have all of these skills and attributes. So how do we ensure we get them in our project? You can work to develop the skills in yourself, but you can also use your team. Lean Six Sigma is very rarely done only by individuals in isolation. Using a team, run by the Green or Black Belt, we get more views, more solutions, more people involved and overall, a better project. It also means that if the Green or Black Belt is missing some key skills or attributes, they can bring them in from their team.

Conflict management
To resolve issues.

Time and Project Management
To get things done on time.

Facilitation
To run teams, workshops and meetings.

Analytical
To understand situations.

Team building
To get the most from a group.

Selling, motivational and influencing
To ensure people accept change.

Presentational
Able to present to colleagues from most junior to most senior level.

Mentoring and coaching
To pass on knowledge.

Listening and questioning
To find out as much as possible.

Lean Six Sigma Tools
Understand and be able to use.

Change Management
and how to implement it.

> "... bump, bump, bump, on the back of his head, behind Christopher Robin.
>
> It is, as far as he knows, the only way to come downstairs but sometimes he feels that there really is a better way, if only he could stop bumping for a moment and think about it."
>
> ## A. A. MILNE

Winnie the Pooh cannot think of a better way to get down the stairs, because he is too concerned about the constant bump, bump, bump on the back of his head. He needs space to stop and think.

Being a Lean Six Sigma Green or Black Belt gives us time to pause and reflect on what is happening around us. After that, we can provide a structure to follow and some ideas to solve problems.

To be a successful Green or Black Belt, you need many soft skills as well as the hard technical tools of Lean Six Sigma. It's hard work to develop the soft skills but once you have them, the rewards are worthwhile to your status as a successful Belt and to your career prospects.

4.3 How to be an effective Green or Black Belt

Over the last 30 years of training and coaching Lean Six Sigma Green Belts and Black Belts as well as Lean experts, I have discovered that to be effective takes 2 distinct skillsets. Firstly, you must be very good at running projects, identifying root causes and generating solutions. I have worked with people who have come up with quality solutions to majorly complex issues all over the world.

However, they have been frustrated and annoyed that their business never implemented these solutions, even though they would solve major strategic problems. Or, they were implemented partly or for a short period only to fail. This is where the second skillset is crucial. The ability to get your organisation, colleagues and or management to accept your solution. If you can do that, then your quality solution will be implemented fully and your solution embedded in your organisation brings the predicted benefits and major changes you wished.

WITHOUT ACCEPTANCE, NOTHING CHANGES

The issue is, how many companies or training organisations or consultancies give equal weighting to both parts of the equation? How many of us spend as long in our training program talking about change, influencing, teamworking, motivation, rapport, communications, facilitation, presentations, understanding change in general as we do teaching stats or 5S or problem-solving tools and techniques?

You can come up with the greatest solution to a problem in the world but if nobody accepts it, then it has been a waste of time and your Green Belt or Black Belts will get frustrated and the organisation will start to question Lean Six Sigma or your approach.

Let's illustrate the power of this equation. A Black Belt is trained and spends time setting up a project, collecting data robustly, identifying root causes and developing a fantastic solution. Herself, her team and her sponsor, with the support of their MBB, have developed an almost perfect solution. Let's give it 9 out of 10.

However, they spent little time working with those affected, didn't communicate what was happening and why, almost alienated the managers in the problem area and so their level of acceptance was 3 out of 10. This, therefore, gives them a 27% chance of total success.

She then works with her Master Black Belt to try and work out why it has not been accepted and they believe that it is due to the fact that the solutions were not perfect and that something was missing. They work on it and make it perfect so get a 10 out of 10 score but with the acceptance at 3, she would still only have a 30% chance of success. Hours and hours are spent making the perfect solution, with virtually no difference to its chances of success.

If instead, the Master Black Belt, Black Belt, the sponsor and her team put extra effort into the acceptance element, working with people, communicating, influencing and engaging with them, allaying fears, and she manages to increase her score to 8 out of ten, then her chances of success move from 27% to 72%.

It is clear where the effort needs to take place for any Lean Six Sigma project to be a success.

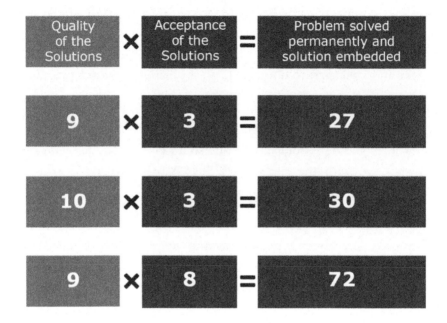

It is my belief that many of us in the Lean Six Sigma world are obsessed with the technical part of the equation and almost just expect the acceptance part to happen.

When you read Lean Six Sigma books, they are all about technical skills and virtually nothing is written about the acceptance part of the equation.

We then wonder why solutions are not accepted. We just assume that we will build it and they will accept it without any questions, without deep explanations or convincing those involved that this is the best option. Green or Black Belts are sold on the notion that if they solve problems, then they will be heroes saving the day. However, without acceptance, they can't be heroes so get frustrated and disillusioned.

I wanted however to check my belief that we spend most of our time teaching the technical aspects of Lean Six Sigma was true so I did a survey.

I conducted a survey of 27 suppliers who showed up on the first few pages of Google for Lean Six Sigma Black Belt training. I excluded 100% Effective Ltd (my company) from the results and what I discovered was that I was indeed correct. We focus on the technical aspects. What did the results show?

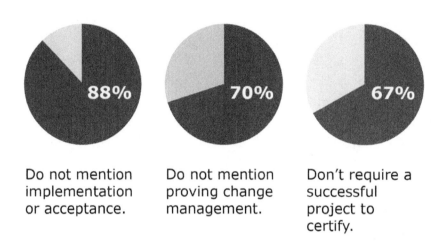

88%	70%	67%
Do not mention implementation or acceptance.	Do not mention proving change management.	Don't require a successful project to certify.

The first element I looked at was what each provider said on their web pages about Lean Six Sigma Black Belt training, what was covered, what was important and their emphasis for the course. 88% of programs I looked at didn't mention implementation, change or acceptance as being part of Lean Six Sigma in any way. They didn't make any mention that you had to apply the learning at any point. They only gave a quick overview of Lean Six Sigma and listed some tools.

Now I know this is not perfect as a survey, but I looked at the Google results incognito so included sites in the UK and the US. I then looked at the content of their training courses as they listed them. Most had a nice long list of all the topics that were covered. 70% of suppliers have no mention of proving any training in Change Management, influencing or any aspect of how to ensure acceptance of a solution in any way. Only technical skills.

Of the 30% that did mention some kind of change management or softer skills, only 1 had any real change management aspect to their training, which was a 3-day change management module at the end of the training. The others mentioned a couple of tools such as stakeholder analysis or communications planning but nothing which would actually provide any balance with our equation. Nothing which would really support acceptance of solutions.

I then thought that, although they don't teach it or talk about it, perhaps they ensure that people have applied the learning to certify. Amazingly, 67% of providers don't ask for a project to be completed to obtain certification. That means at best, 67% of those who certify in Lean Six Sigma as Black Belts have never had to apply their learning to a real-life project. They might never have applied the learning. All they have done is learnt the technical tools and regurgitated the theory.

Of course, some of these Black Belts will have gone on to apply the learning but they have not been tested to make sure they are doing so effectively. I think this is very revealing; if we don't teach both sides of the equation, then how can people learn to ensure the solutions are accepted in the organisation?

4.4 Project Selection

After selecting your Green or Black Belts, the next area that you must concentrate on is selecting the project or problem to solve. It is essential that this is done correctly, as failure to do so will have a major effect on our deployment and success. It is very easy to send delegates onto training and just ask them to bring a project with them. This is totally unfair as they have no idea what Lean Six Sigma is or what they are required to do during the training. We see this happen time and time again: delegates get an email which says, 'please attend the training on the following dates and please bring with you a project of problem to solve'.

Any company that goes down this path proves that this is not a strategic deployment and is in fact just a manager wishing to train their people. This of course might not be an issue, learning the skills, tools and the Lean Six Sigma approach is worth it. However, you can't then hold the people accountable for the success of their projects. If you are truly looking to obtain all the major benefits of Lean Six Sigma, then you must think strategically. You are freeing up your best people for a large number of days – would you not want them to work on your strategic problems? You have engaged with a training company or consultancy – would you not want them supporting your best people to solve problems that will have an impact on your business? We must plan and select the problems that need to be solved. Failure to do so is, in fact, an abdication of responsibility.

Project selection should be conducted by the executive team or at least they should make the final decision as to what projects are worked on. This requires your executive team and other senior managers to have an understanding of Lean Six Sigma and what is required for success. As such, they should have undertaken Champion Training. In many instances, during the champion training, your consultancy or training partner would discuss with your executive team which projects could be run or which problems need to be solved. In order to do this, it requires a business to:

- Understand their current position
- Have robust and reliable data to assess what needs to be improved
- An understanding of the Voice of the Customer
- A strategy or strategic direction

It may sound crazy that a business would not understand or have this data but unfortunately, it is amazing how often this is not the case. Later, we can discuss how to collect the information needed to select a problem of the project but first let's look at the best process to select the project.

Over the years, we have seen many processes used. However, it is our opinion that the best approach would be to have a hopper full of identified projects ready to be solved. This hopper would obtain suggestions for projects from a large number of routes. They could come from sources including:

- Health and Safety – The first port of call for improvement projects or problems would be issues raised associated with near misses or incidents. This lets us use Lean Six Sigma to remove or mitigate these issues.
- Complaints – Written, verbal or via your emails and social media channels. A person should be constantly monitoring all of these areas to identify common issues which are not being addressed. They should then be investigated and added to our problem hopper.
- Voice of the customer analysis – Your marketing team and others should be regularly talking to customers and understanding what is important to them. You should then review your current product and service and identify problems that should be addressed.
- Competitor Analysis – Again, marketing should be assessing what our competition direct and indirect are doing. This should identify problems and opportunities which may lead to projects being solved.
- Quality issues – Our quality department should of course be collecting data on a daily basis about where problems exist, what mistakes are made, the time and money lost as a result of them and hence be able to instantly tell us what should be improved.
- Finance team – Their role is to identify where we are not being as effective as we should be. Where we are reworking items, where our costs are too high, where we are wasting time on

overtime, etc. Any cost in the business that is not optimum would give us an opportunity for an improvement activity. Anywhere that too much time is spent would be an opportunity.

- Engineering/design – When they analyse the build or development of our products or services, they should be looking for ways to standardise products, parts, etc. and as such, should suggest areas to be improved.

- Our staff – Once we have given them all training in items such as the 8 wastes, standardisation and removal of variation, we would expect staff to suggest areas where we could improve. Although I am not a fan of them, employee suggestion schemes might be a route. I am not a fan as I think it should be part of an employee's day-to-day life to suggest and solve issues, not something which is written down and passed on to others.

- Strategic reviews – When our executive team develops the strategy for the year, they must identify areas where we need to vastly improve. This obviously provides us with improvement requirements.

- Purchasing – Analysis of the different parts we purchase, multiple purchases of scrapped parts, costly components, poor quality components or late deliveries should all be monitored by procurement and provide excellent project ideas.

- HR – As they review the performance and requirements of our people, it will become obvious where we have issues with motivation, training, pressure, stress, etc. and they would show us opportunities to improve.

- Customer suggestions – If we listen to our customers, they provide us with areas of concern but also ideas to improve. We need to have a process to capture these ideas and feed them into our hopper.

- Supplier suggestions – Our supplier also constantly tells us ways to be more efficient, reduce costs and improve quality.

Again, a process needs to be in place to collect and monitor these ideas.

- IT – Our website and FAQ pages are great sources of issues. If a frequently asked page is constantly reviewed, this suggests there may be issues with our instructions or our products we should monitor and report. Likewise, our website performance data may provide sources of projects.

I am sure there are other sources of problems in a business or opportunities to improve but if you had all of these departments and people sending ideas to your project selection hopper, then you can start to identify the best ones to work on. By developing a formal project selection process, we can ensure that our best people are working on the most important projects and allocate them appropriately.

The decisions are made by the executive team. However, they do not have time to review and assess the hundreds of potential problems. This should be done prior to their decision- making meeting. The assessment should take 2 steps. Firstly, each idea should be investigated, some simple data collected so the scale and severity of the problem can be assessed, and then the potential benefits reviewed. This should be done by your Master Black Belts. They would use a simple data collection format to review and then document each potential problem. When you first start this process, it can be daunting as you will literally be swamped with suggestions for improvements. As a result, it becomes even more important that you have a process. It is also important that you include the people suggesting the ideas in data collection steps and even more so that you feedback results of the investigation to them.

PROBLEM HOPPER SOURCES

Health and Safety
The first port of call for improvement projects or problems associated with near misses or incidents.

Complaints
Monitor written, verbal or via email and social media channels.

Voice of the Customer
Regularly talk to customers and understand what is important to them.

Competitor Analysis
Assess what competitors are doing and identify opportunities.

Quality
Collect data about where problems exist, what mistakes are made, and time and money lost.

Finance
Identify costs in the business that are not optimal.

Engineering
Analyse the development of products or services to find ways to standardise them.

Staff
Once trained in the 8 Wastes, encourage staff to suggest areas for improvement.

Strategic Reviews
The executive team develops an annual strategy, identifying areas to improve.

Purchasing
Analyse costly or poor quality components, or late deliveries to identify improvement opportunities.

Human Resources
Review performance and requirements to reveal issues with motivation, training, and stress.

Customer Feedback
Customers make suggestions and provide ideas for improvement.

Supplier Feedback
Suppliers constantly tell us ways to be more efficient, reduce costs and improve quality.

I.T.
Constant review of FAQs suggests issues with instructions or products.

If you don't keep the people who have suggested the ideas in the loop, why would they suggest ideas again? If you don't have a process to effectively collect ideas, they will be missed and opportunity lost. I recall a telecommunications company we worked with a few years ago. Their Deployment Champion told us about a story that could have cost the company millions of pounds or dollars. They held a workshop with part of the business and during that workshop, they asked people for ideas of how they could improve. The ideas were captured on a flipchart and the team dispersed. The team running the workshop were busy and the flipchart was never written up. Essentially, all the ideas were lost. Some months later, our Deployment Champion happened to get into the lift with one of the attendees of the workshop. She asked what had happened with her idea as she had not heard anything or seen any difference in the process. The Deployment Champion truthfully said they had not heard about it but would investigate.

The Deployment Champion did indeed investigate and found the team who had run the workshop. They apologised and eventually found the flip chart. To cut a long story short, they realised how good an idea it was, implemented it, and saved the company a stack of money and improved the quality. The issue was no project identification process. We must have a way of identifying problems and then collecting basic data to assess them. Thankfully, in our telecommunications company, not only did the person suggesting the idea follow this up but the Deployment Champion took it seriously. This was just luck as, in most companies, the ideas are not only lost but the person suggesting them is so hacked off they never suggest anything again.

If we do have that initial data collection process working, what we end up with is a whole list of opportunities. We now need to filter them down so that we can provide some data to our executive team so they can select the ones to work on. This could be done by the Master Black Belt or the Deployment Champion. We would suggest that again, a process is used so that all opportunities are given equal assessment. It could be that you use a prioritisation matrix as shown below:

ID	PROJECT TITLE	Status	BENEFIT					EFFORT					RECOMMENDED PRIORITY
			Revenue Enhancement	Operating Profit (from Cost Reduction)	Capital Reduction	Strategic/ Other Benefits (Cycle Time Reduction, Customer Satisfaction, Employee Retention, Cost / Capital Avoidance)	TOTAL BENEFIT	Personnel Requirements (average FTE)	Project Duration (wks)	Capital Requirements ($MM)	Project Risk (None, Low, Medium, High, VeryHigh)	TOTAL EFFORT	
	Importance Weighting:		0.25	0.25	0.25	0.25	1.00	0.25	0.25	0.25	0.25	1.00	
1	Project A		1	3	9	1	3.5	3	3	9	3	4.5	
2	Project B		3	9	1	1	3.5	9	3	2	3	4.3	
3	Project C		9	9	3	9	7.5	1	3	1	1	1.5	
4							-					-	
5							-					-	
6							-					-	
7							-					-	
8							-					-	
9							-					-	
10							-					-	
11							-					-	
12							-					-	
13							-					-	

Each project is listed and then is assessed against the benefits it would bring and the effort to solve them. In fact, you could use any kind of assessment, as long as you are consistent. Some companies will add cost, time, etc. as criteria to assess their project. Each assessment is provided with a weighting as not all areas are equal and then, through some simple maths, you can prioritise each project idea against each other. You can then plot them on a graph and see the projects which would give the best benefits to your company. It is important that you are consistent and document the scale for your scoring.

You can now attend your monthly steering committee and present to them the top areas for improvement. The executive team would then identify which problems to work on. As they know which ones will aid their strategy, you ensure that your best people are working on the most important problems. As a result, when people turn up for training, they have been assigned a project and solving it will have a major impact on the business.

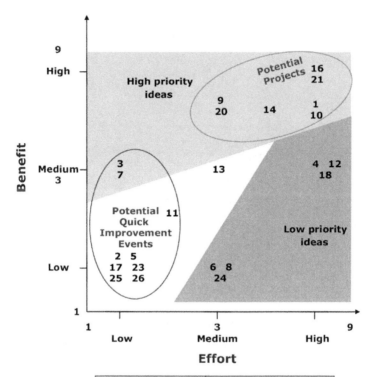

	Benefit	Effort
Low	Will positively impact local team's speed/quality/cost but not wider function	Affects a single team or discipline area, needs a core team of =< 5, and can be completed in under 3 months
Medium	Will positively impact speed/quality/cost of 2012 goals (and beyond)	Affects more than one discipline but is entirely within function, needs a core team of more than 5 people, or needs >3 but <9 months to complete
High	Must do to support 2012 goals (and beyond) , and impact is sustainable	Scope stretches beyond function, or will take >9 months to complete

It is true to say that we must also assess which resources we have available, how much time they have and if they have the capability to solve this issue. So, it is not always as straightforward as this suggests. It becomes a little bit like 3-dimensional chess, but it does mean making informed decisions that are best for the company.

A word of caution: when you only have a few Green or Black Belts, you must let them finish their current project before giving them another one. The more we overload our staff the less they complete and the result is our benefits are delayed from coming to the fore.

As Little's Law shows, the more we work on a project, the longer it takes to complete it.

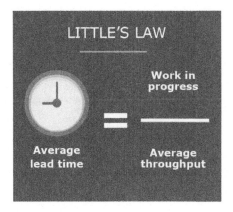

Our process for project selection therefore has a hopper full of potential ideas, which are then filtered to suggest the priority. We only release the next project to be worked on when our Green or Black Belt have completed their last priority. Our process is robust, data-driven and can be communicated. You can tell people why their idea has not been used yet and keep them up to date with progress. It also means that we can start to allocate smaller projects, perhaps to Yellow Belts, so that we can get more projects completed. As well as that, it provides our executive team with data to assess if they need to invest in more training, use of contractors or external resources, as they can see what the benefits would be.

THE VALUE OF LEAD TIME
IN A PROJECT ENVIRONMENT

You have	Each needs	There are

8 projects	15 man-months of effort to complete	4 project managers

TRADITIONAL APPROACH

Resources spread:
Results accrue at the end

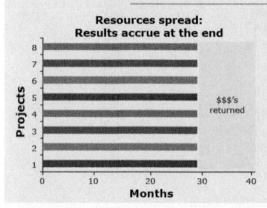

$$$'s returned

Start all projects at once, having each project manager manage two projects in parallel.

PULL APPROACH

Resources spread:
Results accrue at the end

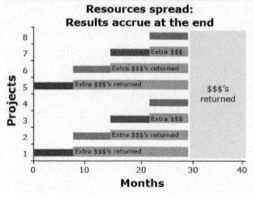

$$$'s returned

Two project managers on the two highest priority projects until they are completed (7.5 months.)

Unfortunately, most companies don't have this level of project selection sophistication. Each manager is left to make decisions on their part of the business and what should be improved. They are allowed to deploy their talented resources as they see fit, mostly based on gut feel, a limited view of the business and to make them look good, or cover up mistakes. If we are truly a process-driven company where we look at processes from end to end, then we must review the use of our talent in the same way. Introducing a robust project selection process at company level will ensure that our Green and Black Belts provide the best return on investment for the business. Let managers use Yellow Belts to run local improvement projects but ensure they are monitored through our Lean Six Sigma hopper.

4.5 Key change questions for every stage of a Lean Six Sigma project

Change management is something you should be thinking about at every stage of your implementation and project so that your solutions are accepted into your organisation. Effective Green and Black Belts will use Change tools and think about change at each stage of DMAIC.

To make this easier, we've identified questions you should be asking yourself at each stage of an improvement project.

Define Phase

This is the very start of your project, so is the first place you can get it wrong. Mistakes, miscommunications or mistrust at this stage can be difficult to correct later on. Whether correctly or not, first impressions tend to stick, so you need to tread carefully at this early stage to prevent long term problems.

You must ask yourself:

- Do you understand all the key stakeholders affected by, or involved, with your problem?
- Do you understand each stakeholder's current position and why they are in this position?
- Do you have a strategy to engage, convince and communicate with each key stakeholder?
- Do you, your team and your sponsor all agree and fully understand the problem you are tackling and the consequences of not solving it?
- Have you developed a simple communication to explain the problem to different levels in the organisation so they are aware of what you are doing, why and how?
- Is each stakeholder group represented in your team, or been told they will need to provide some time to assist you?
- Have you set up a communications plan so that everyone who needs to be regularly communicated to, will be?
- Have you set up a mechanism to obtain regular feedback from each stakeholder group?
- Do you have a process to review feedback and communicate back to stakeholders what has happened as a result of their feedback?
- Have you delivered a short explanation about the problem to the people affected in order to engage them?
- Can you deliver an elevator speech to explain the problem and its consequences?

Measure Phase

Excellent communications at the Measure phase are essential, as you will need the cooperation and support of the people directly involved in the process you are looking to improve in order to collect the data you need. Working with people, training them and being respectful of their superior knowledge of their role in the process is key. You should ask yourself these questions:

- For those who you have asked to collect data, have you developed a simple explanation of why they are doing it and why it is important?
- Have you trained them in how you want the data collected?
- Have you talked to the managers in the areas where data will be collected?
- Have you communicated an update of the problem to the whole company, via a consistent format?
- Can you easily explain how the data was collected, and prove it is robust?
- Have you developed graphical and logical formats to share the data you have collected?
- Have you delivered a short explanation about the size of the problem to the people affected so they are involved and engaged?
- Can you deliver an elevator speech to explain the problem, its consequences and the exact size and scale of the issue?

Analyse Phase

Navigating the Analyse phase can be tricky, as this is the phase where the cause of the problem is identified. For those personally involved in the process, the cause of the problem can feel a lot like blame is being assigned, so it is not unusual for Lean Six Sigma leaders to meet resistance or face challenges at this stage when everything has run smoothly to this point.

It is worth remembering that individuals, teams or departments are not responsible or to blame for a problem, regardless of the root cause, as everyone is working to the best of their ability within the confines of their role.

These are key questions to ask yourself in this phase:

- Have you communicated the root causes to managers or workforces who are affected by them, or are responsible for them?
- Have you communicated an update of the problem, avoiding assigning blame, to the whole company, via a consistent format?
- Can you easily explain how you identified the root causes from the data you collected?
- Have you reassured people that there will be no disciplinary action or kickback as a result of identifying the root causes?
- Have you developed graphical and logical formats to share the root causes, with the data to prove it?
- Have you delivered a short explanation about the size of the problem, and the root causes identified to the people affected so they are involved and engaged?
- Can you deliver an elevator speech to explain the problem, its consequences, its size and scale, and what the root causes are?

Improve Phase

The Improve phase can be one of the most exciting in a Lean Six Sigma project, particularly if you've already got the people involved in the change and the process on your side. It's a time of momentum and excitement for the improvement. However, it can also be the time when people dig their heels in, procrastinate or flat out refuse to implement an improvement. To help avoid this, ask yourself these key questions:

- Have you invited ideas on potential solutions from all the areas affected by the problem?
- Have you invited solutions from other areas of the business, and outside, if you can?
- How have you put a plan in place to make your solutions creative?

- Can you explain why you chose the solutions you have, and how you did this?
- Have you identified how different people or groups may react to the solutions and made plans to address any issues?
- Prior to testing or piloting the solution, have you explained it to all stakeholders so you can obtain feedback during the pilot?
- Have you talked to all managers affected by the new solution so you fully understand issues, restrictions and constraints?
- For each group you have to convince, have you identified the benefits to them and explained them in a calm, congenial manner that they will understand?
- Have you developed a convincing sales document for each level in the business, and developed that into a number of different presentations?
- Have you planned your pilot or testing so that you can obtain feedback and change the solution if required?
- For each group or person affected, have you documented what is important to them, what their fears may be, how they will have to be supported?
- For each group or person affected, have you communicated with them in small groups or one-to-one?
- Have you developed a training or support plan for each person?
- Have you set up the environment so that mistakes are accepted and lessons learned without recriminations?
- Have you communicated an update of the problem, and how the solution will work, to the whole company, via a consistent format?

Control Phase

Often an afterthought, the Control phase should be anything but. As people are now actually using your solution, communication and support are more important than ever. While your testing and pilot should have picked up any issues, you ought to still be listening hard to ensure everything is working as it should. Plus, a little gratitude goes a long way; where people have made changes or faced disruption, it's important to recognise that so they feel valued. You should ask yourself these questions:

- Have you trained everyone using the new solution?
- Can you prove they all have the ability to use the new solution?
- Have you looked for other opportunities to use the solution in the business?
- Have you run a lessons learned session?
- Have you contacted all those involved, and their managers, to thank them for their hard work and support?
- Have you posted an update of the problem to the whole company, via a consistent format?
- Have you written up your project so others can learn from it?

Conclusion

Lean Six Sigma is a proven methodology that provides real results and leads to permanent improvement. But the success of Lean Six Sigma is down to those who deliver training and run projects to remember the importance of gaining acceptance. Quality and acceptance are equally important; without investing time in both, your solution will not work as it should.

Ultimately, it's important to remember that people make up all businesses and so, running a project will always be an exercise in dealing with people. If you work with them, instead of fighting them at every step, you have a greater chance of success.

But more than this, we should know that Lean Six Sigma is more than a set of technical tools. It has the power to be flexible and change to suit the needs of the organisation; it should not be a rigid set of rules, but a set of guidelines to lead us in the right direction.

By ensuring both sides of your quality and acceptance equation are balanced, and putting your focus on people and processes, you can ensure your Lean Six Sigma solutions stick every time.

4.6 How to train effectively – Blended Learning

COVID-19 and the year 2020/21 have shown us that the world has changed. That is true in the training as with everything else. For any Lean Six Sigma program to be effective, we must train and educate people from the top down. This means that we must use the most effective way possible. Traditionally, companies would send all of their people on classroom training events for Champion training (leadership team knowledge), Yellow, Green and Black Belt training. This training would, in some cases, take place over weeks. For any purists out there, Black Belt training takes 4 weeks in a classroom to complete.

We believe that there are several issues with this training approach. Typically, this kind of training covers every subject in the Lean Six Sigma Book of Knowledge you can cram into your classroom training time. This means that you will cover subjects which you may never use, which is a pointless exercise as we all know that unless you use and apply your training, you will not retain or understand it. In terms of support, you would be left with a manual, your notes and your memories. For some, this will be enough, so that when they come to need the training or the tool, they can remember or look at their notes and be reacquainted with the subject. However, the vast majority of people just look at the pages and are lost.

Classroom training is also only as good as the trainer you have for the day or days you have them. Most of the training companies in the market today are generalists so the trainer you have will have limited experience in Business Improvement. The training is also very one dimensional in that the trainer will use slides and a flipchart to teach you, with the odd exercise thrown in. They don't hit all the learning styles so unless you are one of the people who can learn in this way, you are lost.

Lots of people, when they start to apply Lean Six Sigma, realise that they have new questions, new challenges and a new understanding of the subject. As such, they need to ask new questions and get support to use the approach and the tools. Without coaching, people stumble and make mistakes, miss opportunities or get frustrated and stop. Traditional classroom training stops at the end of the training. This is not an effective method to learn a subject and be effective.

Lastly, as we said earlier in this book, if you are only assessed on your ability to regurgitate facts by completing a multiple-choice, open-book exam, then you have never had the joy of applying your learning and really proven to yourself and others that you now have knowledge.

For your deployment to be effective, you must have educated and knowledgeable people. To do this, we must change the methods and content of our training. We have already talked about the content of effective training so now let's look at the training methods.

The only truly effective way to train your staff is through adapting and engaging in what is called Blended Learning.

Research by a consortium of universities has highlighted the enhanced learning outcomes seen in blended learning when compared to traditional classroom teaching methods.

Ten lecturers and 40 students from Tampere University of Applied Sciences (Finland), the University of Lincoln (United Kingdom), the University of Vic (Spain), Liepaja University (Latvia) and HKU Hilversum (Netherlands) collaborated on a project they called Media Culture 2020.

The aim of the project was to develop joint multidisciplinary courses using traditional learning approaches in the form of 2 two-week workshops, supported by online teaching, virtual group discussions and use of social media platforms.

In their research paper, lead authors Richard Vickers and James Field from the University of Lincoln, and Cai Melakoski from Tampere University of Applied Sciences, said: "The blend of both synchronous and asynchronous teaching methods fostered an open, blended learning environment, one that extended the traditional boundaries of the classroom."

Blended learning is the most effective way for an individual to learn and the most cost-effective way for a company to pay for training. It is now recognised that most training programs in the world will become blended. The use of technology, social media, COVID-19 and the lack of time we all suffer from has transformed the training environment over the last few years. Blended learning allows you to quickly, and at a time to suit you, learn from online training, pre-reading, virtual classrooms, coaching, case studies, peer to peer discussions, etc. You attend virtual classrooms to work in groups and learn how to apply the learning. Every person in the virtual classroom is at the same level of understanding so learning is quicker and more effective and you can discuss in detail how to do the learning. You can obtain all the benefits of the classroom – discussions, working in teams, getting instant feedback and hearing the questions of others but in a far more effective manner.

As Business Improvement experts, blended learning works for us as we realise that classroom training has inherent waste and variation built into it. In an effort to apply our own philosophies to our training, we developed our blended training programs. It reduces the time taken to learn, it enables the application of the learning quicker and more effectively and it is based on each individual's needs.

If, like most companies in the world today, you want effective training, then blended is the only way to go. However, to have real blended learning, you must work with a supplier or design your program to include the following:

- Quality interactive, gamifies online training courses
- Access to an online portal
- Virtual or classroom training workshops
- One to one coaching sessions with a Master Black Belt
- Case studies, exercises, discussions and project work
- Ongoing support and lifelong learning

Quality interactive, gamified online training courses

This provides training in subjects to ensure everyone is at the same stage of understanding at the start of a program. You don't want people to waste time learning subjects that they already know, for example, an engineer learning basic statistics. In a traditional classroom, the engineer would sit through a few hours of a trainer explaining to others in the class how to do this. They would watch others struggle and get frustrated as for them this is a waste of time.

With eLearning modules on basic statistics, it's simple: you ask everyone to almost complete pre-work before coming on the training. You give them a list of modules that they must complete. This means that before you start, everyone is on the same page. As students or trainers, there is nothing more frustrating than having one or two in a classroom who are behind the rest. As trainers, we typically must train at the rate of the slowest person in the room. This means that hours and hours are wasted getting them caught up. Online training helps to eliminate this.

Online eLearning also provides us with countless other benefits in our blended training approach. Following the end of the training course, by providing access to the students to the whole course via eLearning, they have the perfect aid memoir. No longer do you have to rely on your notes or memory; you simply log in and take the 20 min of the course again and instantly, you are back up the learning curve and ready to apply your learning. This is amazing as a support mechanism for students. Now we don't mean that they watch a video of the classroom when we say eLearning. This is a very poor way to provide eLearning; the sound is normally poor, subjects are not in content, there is no structure, no interactivity and little engagement. We mean quality interactive eLearning when the student listens to professional voice-overs, not just reading the screen but adding stories and content as they go. On page, we have animations, drag and drop and other interactions with the screen. Countless examples and games.

Complex subjects or advanced subjects also don't need to be taught to everyone. In the classroom model, we would spend hours training people in topics they may never use. With eLearning, we can have them as additional learning. Then, when a student needs to understand and use this topic, they can simply take the online class, learn the topic and talk to their coach (more about this as part of blended below). This means that some topics can be taken out of the training program and thus the time in the virtual or real classroom is reduced for all but those needing the training still get it.

Having an online Lean Six Sigma platform also means that you can set assignments, challenges and exercise for your teams to do. You can provide more examples to work on or work through. In the classroom, we are restricted by time; online, we are not. For those who wish to delve deeper into a subject, they can simply log in and practise the topic with worked examples. Again, learning is enhanced.

Lastly, for some, a classroom environment is scary, non-effective and distracting from day-to-day requirements. In essence, the classroom environment for many is not an effective learning vehicle. Through education, this was the only way to learn; due to learning styles or other behavioural factors, they perhaps didn't learn as much as they could. Online learning changes that: people can learn when they want, can retake a class as many times as they like, stop it and start it to suit their needs. With a coach, they can then ask questions for clarity and suddenly they can learn. They become more effective and our business benefits.

The learning styles mentioned are also important. In eLearning, when developed properly, all learning styles will be taken into account. Theorists can be given extra reading and shown the origin and background information on a subject. Pragmatists can be given examples of how the subject has been applied. Activists can be given assignments to try to use the learning. Reflectors can take all the time they need to assess and assimilate the learning.

Effective eLearning in each subject should demonstrate and support each learning style so that your training is truly effective.

Access to an Online Portal

Blended learning requires a portal where eLearning is accessed but also which can save us time and monitor the progress. Most companies have a Learning and Management System (LMS) for this. A good LMS can be used to support our blended learning in a few ways.

It can enable students to take quizzes and end of course exams. They can be completed when the student has time and they can fit this into their day as required. This frees up time at the end of a classroom course but it also provides us as managers with data. We can see which question the students struggled with, meaning that if lots of students struggle, we know that this is a subject area we must provide more support in. We can see how many times a student had to take an exam to pass. We can provide individual congratulations when they do pass, providing an opportunity for managers to reinforce learning and achievements.

Quizzes at various points of a blended learning process also mean that we can check how progress is going rather than waiting till the end to find out. In a traditional classroom, we would never have time to do this. It also means that individuals are not under pressure as they are with an end of course exam or quiz, typically meaning they do better. They can also self-assess how they are progressing and take more responsibility for their learning.

Our portal also provides us as managers other data that is invaluable. Who has completed which modules, who has taken advanced modules or read extra elements? Who has struggled to find the time so we can approach them on an individual basis to try and help them? We can look at assignments and assess what has been done; in some systems, you can ask for feedback and set tasks on an individual basis. All in all, the portal or LMS provides us with learning data to support our learners.

Virtual or classroom learning workshops

As delegates will have to spend time working on pre-work to ensure everyone is at the same learning level, we have eLearning to cover more advanced subjects and simple assessments can be conducted via our online portal, so the time in the classroom can be vastly reduced. There is an obvious advantage to this in that less time is required en masse away from day-to-day activities. If you are training an entire team, how you release them all at the same time is often an issue, so reducing this is a major benefit. If travelling to another venue, there is the cost and time associated with this which, again, is vastly reduced.

However, the real benefit of blended learning and using eLearning is that the nature of the virtual or classroom can change completely. It can be argued that the real value-added part of any learning is how to apply and use the training. Discussions with peers and experts about what it means to you and practising the use of a tool or approach are the most important parts. We would agree with this assumption. We find that people get far more out of an exercise, game, simulation than listening to a trainer. This is backed up by all academic studies. In a traditional classroom setting, however, we have to teach the theory first and then have little time for the added-value application part of learning. eLearning changes all of that. Prior to a classroom event, we get the student to take an online module on a subject. This means we can spend a short time recapping and then the rest of the time working on how to use and get the most from a tool, approach or subject. The student has more time to debate, discuss the application in their workplace and plan how to do that. We can run simulations, ask students to deliver teach-backs so that they can prove they understand a topic.

As a result, the virtual or classroom sessions become less and less chalk and talk and more discussion and use.

The number of sessions and duration becomes a result of what you wish to teach, how much time you have and the structure and set up in your business. You could do a few hours a week, 1 day a month or a few days at a time – it really is up to you. True blended learning is just that; a flexible and adaptable way to learn, with classroom elements only being one part of how we teach.

One-to-one coaching sessions with a Master Black Belt

As part of the blended training course, we also need to include one-to-one coaching sessions with a Master Black Belt. It provides you with a chance to ask questions and get support for applying your learning. Over the last 21 years, we have found that companies that include one-to-one coaching in their offering to students are far more likely to succeed.

The coaching must be conducted by an experienced Master Black Belt, either face-to-face or virtually. The Master Black Belt can be a company resource or an external; the key is that the delegates get expert coaching.

Why do we say that coaching is essential?

- It will enable delegates to successfully complete your projects, providing Return on Investment and also proof of learning

- It will help them to achieve certification which to most delegates is highly valued as it looks good on their CV or résumé
- It enables them to ask for specific advice on how to make their project a success
- It enables them to ask for further clarification on parts of the training they didn't understand the first time
- It will help them to understand what data to collect and how to collect it and then how to analyse it and draw conclusions
- They will get hands-on assistance with the use of Minitab or other statistical software
- It will assist them by discussing how to implement your solutions and influence key stakeholders to ensure that solutions are embedded in your organisation
- Their solutions will be more robust and complete, leading to more success
- It supports their personal development by giving them a person to bounce ideas off, ask questions they may not ask in the classroom or wish to discuss in an open forum

With one-to-one Master Black Belt coaching, your delegates will complete their projects quicker and with a greater chance of the solution being embedded in the organisation.

We suggest that coaching takes place between virtual training classes so that questions can be asked and progress maintained. One-to-one coaching also provides management with the ability to monitor learning and progress. We would never suggest that a coach shares sensitive or personal information or thoughts from a session but they can provide updates. This is invaluable to the organisation as they push towards deployment.

For coaching to be successful, apart from being delivered by an experienced Master Black Belt, you should also ensure that:

1. You set a time and date for each session and don't let it slip. It is

very easy to let other things take precedence. We find that the sooner you apply learning, the more you will benefit. It is also about personal development, which should be one of the delegate's key drivers, so don't let sessions slip. In fact, many people tell us that having the time and date booked focuses them on completing tasks.

2. Prior to any session, ensure Master Black Belt has an up-to-date storyboard (presentation on your project), your objectives for the session and any questions you want to discuss. That way, the session will be highly efficient as your Master Black Belt will have prepared for your session.

3. Your coach should run your session in a standardised way. Our coaches use the GROW model to run sessions. That way, you know what to expect and they will be successful and efficient.

4. Throughout the session, be open and honest. Ask your coach about areas of the methodologies that you didn't fully understand, talk about data collection and analysis, talk about stakeholders and how to influence them or anything else you need advice with.

5. At the end of the session, you should recap the actions that have been discussed and set the date and time for your next session.

6. Remember that these sessions are perfect to obtain constructive feedback on your personal performance. Use the session to help you with your personal development. People who are committed to personal development are always far more successful than those that aren't. Ask about how you performed in the task, how you come across, and how you conduct yourself, among other things. That way, you can discuss how you can grow and develop.

Coaching is a powerful and essential part of any blended learning. The number of sessions will vary from company to company but we would suggest that Green Belt will need at least 3 sessions and Black Belt 5 sessions.

It is also possible to run group coaching sessions rather than one-to-one sessions. This is a great exercise if you have a group of people who have an issue with a topic or who have struggled with an exam or assignment. The flexibility of blended learning allows us to adapt as we need to provide total learning.

Case studies, exercises, discussions and project work

Another part of blended learning is the ability to set application activities to practise using tools and techniques. We would suggest that as you consolidate learning with virtual or face-to-face classroom training, you set tasks to be completed prior to the next session. You can then monitor them over the LMS or portal. This also might mean setting background reading to be done, videos to be watched, etc.

Many companies also ask that projects are advanced between sessions. This is an excellent way to keep progress towards certification and solving a problem. One-to-one coaching also ties in with this approach, meaning that Green Belts can complete projects in a couple of months and Black Belts in 2 or 3 months.

Ongoing support and lifelong learning

Learning needs to be constant and we ought to provide our delegates with instant and constant support. As such, Blended Learning goes hand in hand with lifelong support. It is no longer acceptable for a training course to be the end of the learning experience. As we know, adult learning requires the following:

- Theory and understanding of skills
- Application of how the skills can be used and why – examples and exercises
- Practice and application of the new skillset in a real-life setting

- Certification of some kind so that there is something in it for the learner as well as for the company. Some form of recognition of the effort is essential
- Time to reflect on the topic and how they can apply it
- Social interaction with peers and internal experts
- Sharing of successes and failures
- Personal reflections and personal development plans
- Engaging and fun elements and content
- Friendly competition/gamification
- Opportunities to continue to learn and develop
- Continual, ongoing, easy to access, secure support

The last point is vital. We need to set up easy and effective ways to support our learners today, tomorrow and for the rest of their careers.

Personal development is essential for every person in business today. We should all be constantly looking to develop our skills, approach and attitudes so that we can be more successful both personally and in business.

People are realising that it is essential to stay up to date with progress in their industry, function and current skillsets. That is why you need to set up support mechanisms and coaches that support them not just today, but going forward in their careers.

The more support they have, the easier it is for them to continually develop and grow. In order to provide lifelong support, we suggest that you include the following within your blended learning

- An identified Master Black Belt that can be emailed or phoned at any time
- Set up a community page on your system about Lean Six Sigma/Business Improvement. This may include social media where possible
- A monthly newsletter for Lean Six Sigma

- Access to templates and guides so people don't have to reinvent the wheel and can share best practices
- A constant stream of updates on the topics and ideas around Lean Six Sigma and Business Improvement – articles, webcasts, videos, etc
- A mechanism for delegates to share projects, successes, lessons learned and feedback with everyone
- Access to other training courses which support Lean Six Sigma

Conclusion

Blended Learning consists of a number of elements that you must design around your needs and capabilities. Any company offering training needs to be able to fulfil these needs. A combination of virtual training, support, coaching, eLearning and application support will provide effective and productive training.

The benefits of Blended Learning summary

- Retention of knowledge – Individuals learn in different ways. Blended learning ensures that every learning style is catered for. Hearing, seeing and experiencing the same content in different ways means that you will retail more knowledge. You will obtain theory, practice on case studies, and practice in real-life situations, teach others, have discussions, take tests, conduct simulations and experiments as well as reading information. All of this leads to greater retention of knowledge compared to either classroom training or e-learning training courses.

- Application of knowledge – As the classroom element of the blended training has been transformed into more of how to apply the knowledge rather than lecturing, with a bit of practise while going at the slowest learners pace, we know that you will have more time thinking and practising how to apply the knowledge. This leads to a better learning experience, quicker return on investment and increased benefits for your company and yourself

- Engage in a total learning experience – As you will be experiencing everything from video to lectures, from researching to applying on projects, from tools to case studies, you get a total learning experience which you can take any time anywhere.

- Review time and time again – As you have access to the whole course for 1 year after your training has ended, you can recap, reacquaint yourself or just revisit the tools, techniques or approaches over and over again. When you are about to use a tool, just check it again before you do so, not in a book but through the training course. Hear the Master Black Belt, see the examples, and if you need to contact the MBB, they will give you a recap over the phone.

- Online training that is available 24/7 from anywhere in the world – for 12 months you can learn what you want when you want to. You are given access to materials from the moment you sign up. You don't have to wait for months until you have time to attend the classroom training.

- Costs are far cheaper than traditional classroom training and the training itself is more effective – you don't have to travel for lots of days for classroom training, you don't have to spend more than a few days out of your business, you don't have to learn at the rate of the slowest learner.

- Better resource utilisation – We know that the biggest hurdle most people have when undertaking training is time out of the office. Blended learning has been designed to give you the training in an effective manner, both in terms of content but also in terms of time. Why spend 10 days out of the office when you only need to spend 5? You 'pull' the Master Black

Belt to you. The classroom training is highly effective as pre-work ensures everyone is at the same standard, everyone has done the theory before they arrive, which means we can concentrate on application rather than lectures. The classroom becomes fun, effective and a worthwhile use of your time.

- Master Black Belts can change their focus – Our whole ethos is about passing on knowledge but also ensuring that this knowledge is and can be used. The classroom sessions and coaching sessions become the mechanism to apply the learning.

- Consistent training delivery – All delegates will be given the same knowledge with no ambiguity; it's the same no matter where you are in the world.

- More flexible – You can pick the time to learn, you can pick the speed you learn. You can even pick the classroom sessions you want to go to. You have the complete flexibility to learn your way.

- Best practice learning – Blended learning has been proven to be the most effective mechanism for adult learning. You can get up to speed and not be intimidated by others, you can take subjects again and again until you get it and if you still don't get it, talk to your coach one-to-one until you do.

- Learn from others – One of the drawbacks of e-learning online training is that you are on your own. You don't hear the questions others ask, you can't discuss things and you can't practise things. This is where our classroom training comes into its own. You have lots of time to practise, apply and discuss topics and tools.

BENEFITS OF BLENDED LEARNING

Retention
Blended learning ensures that every learning style is catered for. Hearing, seeing and experiencing the same content in different ways helps a learner retain more knowledge.

Application
The classroom element of the blended learning focuses on applying the knowledge with opportunities to practise.

Total learning experience
From video to lectures, from researching to practical application, from tools to case studies, learners gain a total learning experience which they can take any time anywhere.

Review
Access to a whole course for a year after the training has ended, enables a learner to recap the tools, techniques or approaches over and over again.

Availability
24/7 access for 12 months from the moment of sign up. A learner can learn what they want, when they want.

Cheaper costs
Learners don't have to travel for classroom training or spend more than a few days away from the business.

Better use of resources
Pre-work ensures everyone is at the same stage before they enter the classroom, meaning they can concentrate on application rather than lectures.

Contextual learning
Teaching is about passing on knowledge and ensuring that it is used. Classroom and coaching sessions become the mechanism to apply the learning with a learner's context.

Consistency
All delegates are given the same knowledge with no ambiguity; it's the same no matter where they are in the world.

Flexibility
Learners have control over the time and pace to learn. They can even pick the classroom sessions they want to go to.

Best practice learning Blended learning has been proven as the most effective mechanism for adult learning, with flexibility in pace and timing to get up to speed and a reduction in intimidation from others.

Peer learning
Learners have time to practise, apply and discuss topics and tools with their peers and instructor during classroom sessions.

4.7 Who to train and when?

It's no secret that Lean Six Sigma projects fail. Even with the highest quality training, the perfect project selection and the best intentions in the world, projects fail to reach targets, are not sustained, and many never even make it off the ground.

Every Lean Six Sigma project is unique, and so there is no one-size-fits-all reason for project failure. However, there is a common theme that can be detected across many projects that fail, and that is lack of support. Writing for the Six Sigma Forum magazine, Janet Young informs us that around 80% of project initiatives fail because of the human variable. For a Lean Six Sigma project to succeed, it needs to be wholeheartedly supported by those around it. Without this support, those implementing the often challenging projects can stumble and fall at the first hurdle. Put simply, without the company's engagement, any progress will not be sustained.

It's an all-too-common story for Lean Six Sigma Belts worldwide. You return to your workplace having completed your Lean Six Sigma training, armed and ready to put to use your new set of skills, tools and techniques. You've identified a problem that would make an ideal Lean Six Sigma project and you can't wait to begin transforming the business for the better.

Unfortunately, your colleagues don't seem to care. And why would they? While you've been away learning all about Lean Six Sigma, they've been back at the office busy with their own workloads and tackling growing to-do lists. It's now up to you to capture your colleagues' attention and then inspire and engage them to support the great changes you are about to implement. And this will be no easy feat.

Not only does this high hurdle slow down the implementation of Lean Six Sigma projects, but it can be dangerously demotivating for a newly trained Belt. Even with external support that your training providers should offer, with little to no internal support available, building buy-in can be a lonely and difficult task. It is, therefore, no surprise that so many Belts give up on their projects and fail to take their training to certification.

There's strength in numbers

In a survey of 180 Six Sigma practitioners, it was found that one of the most common reasons for unsupported Lean Six Sigma initiatives is that businesses only train one type of Belt, most commonly Black Belts; an issue that was particularly prominent in smaller businesses. The result is that management has insufficient knowledge to support projects, process owners don't feel confident about the outcome and project leaders are left feeling overwhelmed.

The solution is to think more strategically about your Lean Six Sigma training and offer courses in a range of roles to as many members of your team as possible. For example, if an employee is undertaking Black Belt training, it would be wise to also invest in a Green Belt to offer project support and to train someone of a senior position to become their Champion. The result will be a united Lean Six Sigma team that supports one another through training and who are ready to hit the ground running on return to the workplace.

Of course, one of the reasons a lack of varied training is a primary issue for small businesses is undoubtedly limited resources. While we are sure such companies would love to increase their chance of project success by training an entire Business Improvement team, it is simply not within their budget. This might also be the situation for larger businesses.

So where do you start to provide Belts with a chance of success? How many should we train? In what order? There are very difficult questions as it depends on a whole host of factors. Your budget, your objectives, how many people you can spare, how much time they will have, the current level of understanding in the business and how fast you want to go. However, let's look at a common approach to training your people.

If you are just starting out on your Business Improvement journey, it is far harder than if you are a mature organisation that has been deploying for years. As you start your journey you need to achieve a few goals as we have discussed in the deployment section of the book. We need to obtain some quick wins; we need to deploy some resources to show to others the benefits and engage them quickly and we need to only bite off what we can chew.

For most smaller businesses or businesses who are starting on their journey we would suggest that one of the deciding factors is how many projects can we realistically run at one time in the business. Remember that senior managers must be able to support them, you will need expert Master Black Belt support for training and coaching and the delegates will need time to run the projects. The vast majority of companies start by identifying a group of 10 of 12 people who will train to Green Belt level.

Selecting these people is vital for success

It is also essential that you choose the correct projects, which we will discuss later, but you also need to make sure senior managers and sponsors are ready to support your Green Belts.

How to select an effective Green or Black Belt

The selection of who to train as your first group of Green of Black Belts is vital. The first projects and training must be a success to keep momentum, prove the approach, finance the rest of the deployment and be used as a way to influence the whole business.

Identifying the best people is hard but saying who should not be included is easy. Too often, we see managers put people on training courses who don't have anything else to do or are between roles. These are obviously not the right people to put on your course as your beacon of light, as your pioneers. Typically, these people are in the position they are in for a reason. Do you really want to pin all your hopes and the chances of solving a strategic problem on people who are not busy or don't have a role? Of course, you don't, so don't do it.

It would be far better to ask yourself or each of your teams; who is the best, who is the person you don't want to lose for even an hour? Who will cause you the most concern if I used them for x% of their time each week? Every manager or team leader knows exactly who these people are. Surely, they are exactly the people we want to be our pioneers or champions. It does of course give us other issues if we do this. We will need to upskill others, perhaps run overtime, managers might have to step in to fill in for them, but surely this is an opportunity for the others to shine.

If you can get these girls and boys, great. If not, you need to start thinking about other key elements needed for our effective Green or Black candidate.

- Are they enthusiastic?
- Are they open-minded?
- Can they influence others?
- Do they have any specific skills, either soft or technical, which would support their use of Lean Six Sigma?
- Are they disciplined enough to follow a structured approach?
- Are they willing to learn and develop?
- Do they have drive and ambition?

Try to pick a group of people from different parts of the business so they can act as ambassadors when they are trained and engaged in Lean Six Sigma. Perhaps try to take some people who might not fit into the above completely but they are highly influential and by getting them on board, you will quickly convince others. It is work considering these types of people as your trainers and the others will be able to influence them to change. If you can convince these types of people, they are worth their weight in gold.

Selecting the right people is important so please give it time and use a process to choose; don't just ask for volunteers or use people who are spare. You are merely setting yourself up to fail from the start.

As such, we would always recommend training in the following order:

- Champion Awareness Training
- Sponsor Training
- Green Belt Training

Champion training should take place first so that senior managers are all on the same page, have agreed on the way forward, have selected the right people and projects and can support and champion the change in the business. Champion training typically takes around 1 day and is a combination of training and workshop to decide on the best approach for their business.

Sponsor training is needed to ensure that the person who is driving the change and has the problem knows how to get the most from their Green or Black Belt. Sponsors need to know the questions to ask, how to run Gate Reviews at the end of each of the DMAIC phases and how to support and drive Green or Black Belts to success. The training takes again 1 day and is all about the role and how to support the Belts. It may be that some senior managers have to attend both Champion and Sponsor training.

Now that the structure and support are in place, you can start your Green Belt training. Ideally, you will use a blended approach as we have discussed and ensured that training includes change management as well as technical skills. If you start the Green Belt training without the sponsor and champion training, then it is inevitable what will happen.

The trainers will be constantly faced with these types of questions and statements:

- I don't have time for this
- How does this fit with my day job?
- Who selected the projects or how can I select a project?
- How does this tie into the objectives of the business?
- What do I have to do?
- When do I need to complete this by?
- Why are we doing Lean Six Sigma?
- Does my manager know their role?
- Who is my sponsor?
- How will I get others to support me to make the changes?
- How can I get others in my team who have no time?
- And so on....

All of these questions and many others should be addressed by the sponsors and champions. We would suggest that at the start of the Green Belt training, the scene is set by them. They explain the whys and hows as well as answering any questions. They should then be visible during the training and at the end to keep answering questions, reassuring trainees and supporting them.

Our team of Green Belts can then be given support and time to learn and complete projects.

Once we have completed our first wave of Green Belt training, we can now start to expand our deployment as we have some success stories, our change management effort will be well underway with communications and engagement. So, we would suggest that more training takes place to cement our progress. Perhaps a second wave of Green Belts is launched. We may also start to train Yellow Belts, but as a minimum, we start some mass general education.

There is one more belt we have not really mentioned as it is not actually a belt but more of awareness. It is called a White Belt and is so-called in order for us to have a consistency of names. The White

Belt is typically an eLearning course that lasts around 1 hour. It explains what Lean Six Sigma is, why it is important, the benefits and the levels and training that will take place.

We would suggest training all your staff to White Belt level. To support companies, we offer this as a FREE eLearning course. By heading to our website www.100pcEffective.com you can sign up all your people and start the education process. It's a great way to begin the cultural change needed in your business. Now, not everyone will take the training, however, it's a major start on your journey.

Once you have trained a few waves of Green Belts, you can start to think about offering some Black Belt training. This is more intense and our suggestion is that 8 to 10 people learn the advanced techniques of the Black Belt. The best people to choose will naturally show themselves from the Green Belt training. Some will show an aptitude for the subject, many will volunteer and as such, you have a highly engaged group who will become your change catalysts and Black Belts.

Some books will suggest that for every hundred people in your organisation you should have X Green Belts and Y Black Belts. However, we find this too formulaic; it just depends on your needs, resources, budgets and capacity.

4.8 Why is certification in Lean Six Sigma essential?

Certifying as a Lean Six Sigma Green or Black Belt would be a very wise investment in time, energy and money for anyone. It makes sense for individuals to upskill personally, as well as companies to invest time and money to certify their people. Earlier in the book, we talked about what certification is and how to certify properly. However, we need to use certification as a way to engage with our people. We all know that to convince people to change, to influence them, there needs to be something in it for them. In a Business Improvement world, we can use certification as one of the benefits to those involved.

Let's review the benefits to individuals of becoming certified (properly) as Green or Black Belts. You can then use this list as you communicate with your staff and try to engage them in Business Improvement.

1. Be at the leading edge of business thinking. Lean Six Sigma is recognised the world over as the number 1 way to improve a business, to make it more effective and to solve your business problems. So, in order to be at the forefront of business thinking in terms of solving business issues, engaging staff and self-motivation then you must understand Lean Six Sigma. Those that don't will very simply be left behind.

2. Lean Six Sigma will make you stand out from the crowd. The issues you solve using Lean Six Sigma will be visible to everyone in the company. The fact that problems are solved permanently and you can show the benefits means senior managers will show an interest in the person who has solved them. Most people who train as a Lean Six Sigma Black Belt will get promoted or at the very worst become well known and respected members of the business.

3. Lean Six Sigma will help you obtain a bonus, promotion or pay rise. The fact that every time you solve a problem you must prove the benefits you have made means that you can always speak with data. One of the key benefits of this is at appraisal time. You can prove how much you saved your company or reduced problems or improved productivity. You can actually put a figure on it. If you can say, 'I cost the company £50K but I saved £1M, then you have a very strong argument for a bonus, pay rise or promotion.

4. Lean Six Sigma will increase your self-worth, your confidence and your enthusiasm. Those who have qualified as a Green or a Black Belt always become more confident. Speaking with data, understanding what is going on, why things happen and the root

causes mean that when you talk to management, you do so with a sense of newfound confidence. When challenged, you have a structure to hold on to, you have data to use as a weapon and as such, you are less intimidated and your confidence grows. You can see the difference you have made to a company or individuals and know that it was your contribution which did that, making you feel more inspired. You see that the ideas you come up with get implemented, people talk about you in glowing terms, you get mentioned in dispatches and people know who you are, which leads to motivation and enthusiasm that many have dimmed. All in all, successful Belts will feel different, act different and demand more of themselves and their companies.

5. Lean Six Sigma qualifications are applicable in any industry or function. Every industry understands Lean Six Sigma and is using the approach so your new skills will be applicable in any industry or function. Enable you to change roles, business or industry. Lean Six Sigma is seen as a massive benefit no matter your sector.

6. Lean Six Sigma qualifications are recognised worldwide. Certified Black or Green Belt skills are understood all over the globe. It doesn't matter if you work in China, the USA or Brazil, everyone values anyone with Lean Six Sigma on their CV. So, qualifying in Lean Six Sigma gives you a global qualification.

7. Lean Six Sigma enables you to lead change and improvement in your business. It incorporates all aspects of continuous improvement as well as employee engagement and motivation. As such, you will be able to identify where the issues are in a business but more importantly, do something about it. A qualification in Lean Six Sigma includes all the tools and techniques needed to solve problems but also to implement change in a business

8. Lean Six Sigma enables you to obtain quick wins in any business. Using techniques like Kaizen, you will be able to show instant benefits to the business by applying these techniques

9. You will be able to improve customer service. Lean Six Sigma has the customer at its heart so qualifying in Lean Six Sigma means that you will look at everything from a customer's perspective. You will work on improving a client's experience and you will be able to show this to others.

10. You will be able to transform your business. You can be the hero in your business. You can turn a business with high costs or poor productivity around by applying your learning. You can save jobs, save companies and improve morale in the business.

Put simply, Lean Six Sigma qualifications will make a difference in people's lives. We can use this as just one of the ways to influence our people to engage in Business Improvement.

4.9 Selecting the best partner for your training and support

As we have seen, much of the Business Improvement journey requires expert support particularly at the beginning, so how do you select your training and support partner? The choice is vital as they will support your deployment development and the development of your people. They will be the ones providing you with the mechanism to change your culture and improve your current position.

The partner you choose will be determined by many things, including the budget, but this section is designed to give you other areas to investigate and think about when selecting a training and deployment partner for your business.

No matter what you are purchasing for your company, we know how hard it is. Lean Six Sigma training is harder than most. There are providers who can offer you Black Belt training in a few hours for less than £19 or you can select a different company that says in theory the same training will take 20 days and cost almost £10,000. With so many providers and so many ways of delivering courses, it can be tough to work out what you're actually getting and how good they are.

For most of us, it comes down to price, which seems straightforward enough. After all, a Black Belt course is a Black Belt course, isn't it? So why would you pay more than you need to?

However, not all training courses are created equal, so let's look into why.

Firstly, the key question is how much of the deployment, training, coaching, etc. do you have internal capacity and expertise to deliver yourself? If you have Master Black Belts and training materials, then perhaps you just need some support to deliver the training. If that is the case, you need to make a decision on face-to-face, virtual, eLearning or blended. If however, you don't have internal resources, then you will need to find a partner who can provide more than just the odd training course.

Most major consultancies provide support to clients but are they experts in training and delivery? Can they provide full blended learning?

Some questions to use to compare suppliers:

- Can they offer Blended Learning?
- Are they experts in their field?
- Is support available to learners?
- How do they certify students?
- Price?
- Review demos?
- Talk to their team, not just the Master Black Belt or senior partner; after all, they will not be delivering the training for you.
- Do I need a consultant or a trainer?

Can they offer true blended learning as outlined in this book? In order to do this, they must have eLearning, which is where most companies fall. Some will say they have eLearning however, be very wary; it may in fact just be an eBook or slides which you read. Others will have poor quality videos of classroom training they have done in the past.

You also need to examine who developed the eLearning that is included in the offering. For this, there are 2 options. Option one, which is the best, is that the eLearning was developed by the company you are considering. That will mean they have control of it, can adapt it if needed and can give you unlimited access. Option 2 is that the company is buying the eLearning from another company and providing it to you either for a cost or included in your price. Either way, be very wary; companies that resell other people's content are not experts in their subject area, in this case, Lean Six Sigma, so why would you use them and not go directly to the experts?

The next area to compare companies would be that very question; are they experts in their field? If they are, then the likelihood is that Business Improvement or Lean Six Sigma is their main business. Don't buy from training course portal sites. They are masters of nothing but selling and marketing and the likelihood is that support, certification and advice will be almost non-existent. If the company is an expert in its field, you will be able to tell from the following indicators.

- How professional the website is
- Case studies
- The trainers
- Client list
- Articles, blogs, etc.
- Social media

Support is the next area to look into. In a recent survey carried out on eLearning suppliers in the UK, we asked and reviewed the top 26 suppliers of training. Of these, the support provided to clients is quite illuminating. 11% offered some kind of coaching over the phone,

20% said that if you had a question you could email them, and a whopping 69% offered no support at all.

If a company can't or won't provide support to a learner before, during or after the training, then that suggests that they are not experts in their field and they might not be the best solution for you if you don't have your own internal resource.

Training content would be another area to consider. As we have already discussed in some detail, successful training must include change (acceptance) skills and technical skills to ensure problems are solved and permanently in any business. As a result, a good partner would have expertise in both areas. We already shared a recent survey on this which showed that only 12% of suppliers provide this kind of training and that 88% only provide technical training.

You also need to examine the content of the technical training. Lots of training providers only cover very basic content indeed. Although we agree that content needs to be flexible, experts will provide any level of detail needed to suit the needs of their clients. So please check their book of knowledge and who accredits them.

If a company is accredited by a website which only asks for an exam to be passed then again, this is an indication that they are not experts but resellers. You need to find a partner who can help you to train and complete projects. Companies that certify with project submissions have Master Black Belts who can support you as they must be there to review the projects.

Price must become a factor for any training or support. How open and honest is the company you are approaching? How transparent are their prices and how do they charge? If a company charges £29 for a Black Belt course, you have to ask yourself how this can have any credibility. Equally, it doesn't follow that the most expensive is the best. The only way to find out is to review any demos of materials or eLearning on their site and talk to their staff.

Expert Lean Six Sigma providers, when you talk to them, will be able to explain all the elements of this book. They will be able to guide you, support you and give you expert advice. You will not talk to a person with no experience in a call centre, you will talk to a person who is either a Master Black Belt or has years of experience in the industry. You must feel comfortable with your partner so your style and theirs need to match. Your approach and theirs must match. So, give them a ring, ask for a demo, ask lots of questions.

Ultimately, you need to make a decision: do I need a pure trainer or a consultant who can train?

I recently met with a potential client to talk about organising some in-house training and she asked me some revealing questions. She asked about the start and duration of the course, adding: "I don't want a training course which starts at 9:30 or 10 a.m. and finishes at 4 p.m. with an hour for lunch and breaks every hour."

Now, I don't know who they have been using for training but they've been taking the mickey! The other request she had was to make sure the examples and exercises are relevant to her industry and not all about cars. I, of course, told her they would be but it got me thinking about the bigger question. When you get a person to come and train you on a subject, do you want a trainer or a consultant who trains?

First of all, you might ask, what is the difference? In my opinion, a traditional trainer is a person who trains to the materials they have on the course. They stick fairly rigidly to the slides or agenda as they are comfortable in this format. They have some knowledge of the subject but their knowledge stops at the material in hand.

A consultant trainer on the other hand (which is what we employ), is more adaptable as they have been there, seen it and done it. That is to say, they have typically delivered the content of the training operationally; they have real-life experience and they can empathise with the delegates. They are not constrained by the agenda and can, if required, go off-piste for a while and provide more in-depth information on a subject or cover other related topics. They are the kind of people who could run the whole course with a flip chart if the projector failed.

Typically, consulting trainers will work as long as required each day with the client. They will give practical feedback at the end of the session; they will support the learner in any way needed to ensure learning and application of the subject.

Now, not all training courses need a consulting trainer or people with the knowledge I am talking about. Software training, time management, presentation skills and more are delivered by great people who just need to know the material. Lean, Six Sigma, Change Management are topics, in my opinion, that need consultancy trainers to deliver the content.

When you engage an expert company in these areas, you are not just getting a training course but you are being given consultancy at the same time. How to deliver your project, how to solve your problems, how to structure your company for success. Identification of issues and solutions to problems. These elements are the added value items that any consultant would provide when training.

In short, I told our potential client that our delivery personnel are really consultants who train rather than trainers. In my opinion, in the past, she had hired or been exposed to trainers who delivered just the slides in the easiest way possible for them, rather than the best way for the delegates. At 100% Effective, we pride ourselves on the quality of our consultants and the added value they will bring when you engage us in training. So, make sure you get the level of expertise you need when selecting your training partner.

TRAINING
Enlightens
Educates
Empowers
Energises
And helps us to **GROW**

Section 5

How to ensure success, Lean Six Sigma secrets

5.1 Introduction

Many businesses have tried to implement Lean Six Sigma, Lean, Continuous Improvement, Operational Excellence, etc. for decades. Some have been successful and obtained amazing results – GE, Motorola, Toyota, etc. However, many more have failed. Many have blamed the approach, saying things like, 'Lean doesn't work in our industry' or 'Six Sigma is not applicable in service sector companies'. This is obviously untrue because there will always be a company in your industry that has implemented it successfully. What therefore makes some companies successful while others fail?

This has been the subject of countless papers and academic studies over the years. From my perspective, you need to understand why others have failed in order to learn from their mistakes. If you are designing a new program or deployment, then you can learn the mistakes to avoid. However, if you are like many executives, managers, owners and shareholders in companies that have failed, then you should review the other's failures and reflect if you have too succumbed to the same mistakes. Only then can we start to address our shortcomings and redesign our approach to be successful.

In the next section, we will list typical reasons why deployments fail.

Many of the reasons are small but a combination of lots of these reasons will result in a major collapse of your cultural change. After reviewing this list, we will then examine a fundamental area where virtually all programs fail: the human, change management element of business improvement.

5.2 Common reasons your Business Improvement deployment failed

There is a lot of focus placed on how organisations can find the right way to improve their business. The culture of each business is like a unique personality which, while malleable, needs to be respected by your solution of choice. However, we've found that it's not selecting your Business Improvement methodology that's the hard part; it's successfully implementing it.

In our experience, businesses frequently underestimate the barriers to a successful implementation, causing perfectly good Business Improvement methodologies to fail. So, what's causing so many deployments to derail? Here's our rundown of the top ten:

1. Senior managers don't understand what they're signing up for

The buy-in of key senior managers is essential to get a Business Improvement approach signed off. But if they are only aware of the end-goals rather than the work required along the way, enthused members of the C-suite can quickly become disenchanted, with the abandonment of the programme usually not too far behind.

It is essential that we educate senior managers on what Business Improvement and Lean Six Sigma are all about. It is essential that we involve them from the start to design and commit them to the vision for the future. Too often, the senior managers' perception is that it is about everyone else changing in the business when in reality, it should start with them. Walking the talk, showing by example is vital to success.

Senior managers must realise that it's about cultural change and as such, they are the ones responsible for the culture. They must start to behave differently, they must ask different questions, see success differently and in summary, be different than before.

Without senior managers' commitment, buy-in and engagement in any change of culture are impossible. It is therefore paramount that any program starts with senior management and certainly, in the first few steps of deployment, focuses on them. Training, guidance and support will be required for them to change effectively.

2.   You picked the wrong project

People always judge the strength of a Business Improvement programme on the success of the first project. Ensure that the project you pick is neither too easy so it is dismissed nor too challenging so it doesn't reach completion.

The first projects are the ones we will use to promote success to others at all levels in the company. They also, if selected correctly, are the ones that can finance the rest of the program. It is not uncommon for 1 project to finance the rest of the program for 1 year. These first projects are also the ones which we can use to educate people in future training courses. They can be used as templates for success. It is far easier to understand something when it is from your industry and your company than to try to conceptualise it from other sources.

Picking projects which are strategically important but not so large is like trying to solve world peace; it requires a robust, understood and fully utilised process. Develop your process to suit your company needs, let the steering committee determine which ones to work on and in which order.

If you pick the wrong projects, you will open the program up to ridicule and ultimate failure.

3. Your project isn't linked to business strategy

If a project doesn't support the wider business goals, why would managers spend valuable time and resources on it? Just as it is important to consider the size of a project, it is essential to identify how it fits in with the wider strategy to prevent it from becoming sidelined in favour of tasks that will further the business objectives.

Most managers will provide time and resources to a project or task which will enable them to hit their KPIs. Assuming KPIs are aligned to the strategy of the company, then projects must be too. If they are, then managers and sponsors will provide it with full support, they will champion them and make sure the Green or Black Belt has the best chance of success.

4. The candidate is not given the time they need to work on improvement

In order to carry a project through to its successful completion – and actually generate benefits for the company – you need to be given the time and resources necessary. However, all too often project leaders are asked to fit Business Improvement in alongside their other tasks, ensuring it eventually becomes their lowest priority.

Working with an electronics company near London, we trained the senior executives at champion level so they understood and designed the Lean Six Sigma program. We ran a workshop and picked the top 6 strategically important projects to work on and they picked 6 top performers to run those projects. Each person attended and engaged fully with some Lean Six Sigma Green Belt training and they were then each given 4 hours of one-to-one coaching to support the completion of the project and certification. A strong start, I am sure you would agree.

After the training, I went to run the first series of coaching sessions. Each person told me the same story. They were slowly moving forward on their project but they were doing it after work in groups as they were not given any time during the day to work on their projects. As a result, project progress was slow and the guys and girls were getting a little frustrated. I approached the Deployment Champion who said that he knew what I was going to say. "We need to give them more time," and I replied, 'yes'. "OK," he said, "we know we must give them time to solve the problems," and we discussed strategies to free up a few hours per day for each person.

A month passes and back I go to coach them again. Same problems. This time, I went to the board and got them all around the table. I asked them if they were the right people to run the projects, they all said yes. I asked if they had indeed chosen the most strategic projects, to which they all wholeheartedly agreed they had. In fact, many of them were critical to the business. Why then are we not giving them the time to solve these problems? They all agree they would and the strategy to free up the time.

Month three, I meet the guys and girls again. They had made really good progress and in fact, many were almost finished. I asked about time and this is where the issues came out. They had agreed as a group of six to support each other, they worked for hours each night after work and they managed to finish the project, get great results and certify. However, they did it in their own time, for their own certification. They had given up on the business supporting them. The result was that within 4 months, all 6 people had left the business and moved on to bigger and better jobs.

The lack of support and, in this instance, that support was time, meant they were disheartened with the business, resulting in them leaving. The business couldn't get away from focusing on day-to-day activities. They couldn't see how to be strategic as leaders and ultimately, the program failed. If we don't give people time and resources, they may complete the project but you will get nothing else from them. We must remember that this is about change; in the example above, the managers didn't change and the result was a disaster.

We see this problem of not being given time to work on projects regularly. It all comes down to an understanding by senior managers, commitment to the vision and changing behaviour.

    5.   There is no Sponsor or the Sponsor doesn't understand the point

The role of the Sponsor is to grease the wheels within the organisation to ensure that the necessary resources are made available and by communicating with key stakeholders and managers. Without someone effectively carrying out this vital role, the project leader can face too many hurdles for the programme to be a success.

Sponsors in some projects don't exist because the projects were just chosen by the delegates. Sponsors don't understand their role because they will not free up time to learn. Sponsors don't provide support because they don't ultimately believe in the program or the approach. These are issues that appear time and time again.

The result is projects which fail and Green and Black Belts who are not supported. We must insist on Sponsor training so they understand their role and communications from above to explain to them why Business Improvement is so important. If we change KPIs for sponsors, then that would also have an effect.

    6.   Data is unreliable or weak

Your decisions are only as good as your data. If you know that your data is unreliable or incomplete, you can't expect the outcomes to be favourable. However, many programs become unstuck because not enough time is spent gathering data to start with, and without this baseline, you can neither move forwards nor prove any progress you've made.

As we have spoken about throughout the book, one of the key aspects of Business Improvement and Lean Six Sigma is speaking with data. However, this brings with it many problems for our deployment and cultural change. Many managers believe that they have been promoted to their position as they can make the right decisions, particularly when under pressure. As such, they trust their gut. This of course is the complete opposite of a true Lean Six Sigma culture, where we need to prove with data every aspect of the DMAIC process. The result is many managers getting fed up with, rejecting or publicly contradicting the data they have been presented with. This slowly erodes the message and people and teams start to question the approach and it slowly dies. Managers must embrace and accept that the culture will be one of speaking with data. In meetings, when presented with situations and solutions they must ask for and trust the data.

As Disraeli supposedly said, "There are three kinds of lies: lies, damned lies, and statistics."

It is important to realise that statistics can be wrong for many reasons. This may be due to an honest mistake: The maths could have been miscalculated or the sample may not accurately represent the population.

However, they could also be intentionally misleading! For example, individuals can feel so strongly about something that they purposefully only present statistics that support their viewpoint.

For these reasons, it is important to always question the statistics you are given. Ask questions such as where did they come from? Why are they being quoted? Are the numbers correct? Could they be biased in some way?

This is the role of managers, sponsors and champions. If you question your Green and Black Belts about the data they are presenting, then you can ensure that the data is robust and as a result, the decisions you are making are sound. This, however, does mean that you as a manager need to understand the statistics. The problem we see time and time again is that managers don't understand the statistics and either ignore them or don't question them. They will not admit that they don't understand as this is a sign of weakness in some way. We must train, educate and support our managers to question statistics and ask the right questions at the right time.

Most businesses however collect too much data. The problem is that the data is not robust, representative or useful in any way (it was collected for another reason and now you try to use it for your own purposes). Collecting data costs us time and money so we must only collect what we need. Green and Black Belt often struggle during the Measure phase of DMAIC due to a lack of robust data or no data at all. They look at what is currently collected and try to use it to save time. However, they don't check how it was collected or why it was collected in the first place. The result is that poor data is used to represent what is really happening and poor decisions are made, which means typically the problem is not solved and the issue comes back to cause us problems once more.

It is imperative that the correct data is collected, even if it means that problems are not solved as quickly as desired. The key reason in most projects for the delay is the Measure phase and the fact that the Green or Black Belt must set up a robust data collection plan. Managers, executives and leaders must understand the nature of data and data collection and allow time for it to be collected so proper analysis can take place and then complete solutions are implemented.

The collection, use and understanding of data is powerful but can also be extremely dangerous in the hands of people who don't trust it, want to use it or can't wait for it.

7. No one involves the finance department and we don't quantify benefits

If one of your main measures of success is cost-savings, you need to be able to show accurate financial figures. If finance is not involved from the off, they may not have the information they need to rubber-stamp your figures, leaving your significant savings looking a lot less impressive or open to discredit.

In a Lean Six Sigma world, one of the important elements is that we speak with data and as a result, we can prove our benefits and savings. This typically means that any financial savings are signed off by the finance department. Green and Black Belts are encouraged to engage with their finance team to help them identify and quantify any savings. However, if this is not done or the finance department doesn't want to get involved, then they leave themselves open to mockery, discredit or not being taken seriously.

Many Green and Black Belts get this wrong from the start. They don't set up to collect data on the area where benefits will or may come from. As a result, in the end, they can't show the benefits or savings as they have nothing to compare against. They must in their data collection plan measure the size of the problem and the area where savings will come from. Forget to do this and you are doing yourself and the program a disservice.

If you don't know where you started, how will you ever measure how far you've come? Seems pretty simple, doesn't it? But time and time again, we see Lean Six Sigma professionals delivering projects that do not illustrate clearly defined benefits. They're made an improvement, but they can't explain in any tangible way what the impact has been.

It is imperative that they can show the benefits of any project, no matter how small. While it makes a big difference to their ability to certify at the end of the project, more importantly, it can impact the credibility of the organisation. Many people find it hard to quantify the costs or benefits for their project so they don't bother, but I believe that this is a major mistake.

So why do Green and Black Belts struggle to collect data on the benefits? The key reasons are quite simple to explain:

When the project first begins, it isn't well defined – there is just a vague notion of what needs fixing. Working through the Define phase methodically and thoroughly should alleviate this issue.

People don't realise the importance of collecting the current situation data at the start of a project before they have made any changes. Generating this baseline is the only way to re-measure at the end to show the benefits. This tends to lead to performance data rather than data that clearly illustrate the benefits.

It is hard to quantify some of the benefits as the data is weak or badly collected. Belts can be disheartened and fail to collect data they don't think will stand up to scrutiny.

Finance doesn't provide the data necessary, either because they don't collect the information necessary or they don't provide the support to fully understand what the figures mean. For this reason, getting a financial representative involved early in the process is essential.

Before seeing the results of the project, some Belts don't fully understand the importance of the benefits data. This means they don't put the effort into collecting it at the start and by the time they realise it is too late.

Sometimes, it is the political nature of the data that can make a Belt hesitate: it could be related to a reduction in overtime or cutting the headcount. Failing to collect this data may feel 'safer' but it doesn't provide the full picture.

Mostly, however, it is time pressure that prevents a Lean Six Sigma professional from collecting the data necessary. Often, Belts feel pressured to get on with solving the problem rather than collecting data, especially if everyone agrees that the problem exists and is urgent.

There are numerous other reasons I am sure why data is not collected, but the process is absolutely essential.

Consider a recent delegate of mine. She works in the food processing industry and did a fantastic project which would have saved around £1.2M. However, as she'd not collected the necessary data, she couldn't prove it. She knew her savings were significant, but she didn't have robust data to show exactly what had been saved. The delegate was thrilled with the outcome of her project, however, senior management did not recognise her efforts, she did not get the recognition she deserved and it had no impact on her or the outcome of her annual appraisal.

And it's not just the personal impact. If she was not recognised for making such a great contribution to the success of the business with Lean Six Sigma, others may not be encouraged to take training in the future – and the journey towards Business Improvement could derail completely.

If we collect the right data and show the benefits, then it helps us in a variety of ways:

- It helps Belts to get certified
- It helps Belts in appraisals as they can prove the impact they have made on the business
- It helps them be recognised in the business as an achiever
- It helps us to get our solutions implemented as it is obvious what the return on investment will be
- It helps to prove that the investment in Business Improvement is worth it
- It keeps momentum in Business Improvement
- Others can learn from the approach to make it easier for them to solve business issues
- It can be used for PR inside and outside the company

Speaking with data is what Lean Six Sigma is all about. Let's get everyone to recognise the importance of collecting data that stands up to scrutiny and that can be used to enhance the individual's reputation and to drive business improvement in the company. This includes the finance department, which needs to be involved and engaged. Failure to do so is a major mistake in any deployment.

8. Selecting the wrong candidate for Green and Black Belt training

All too often, a candidate is picked for Business Improvement training because they have the time available. For a successful outcome, businesses would be better off selecting a candidate with the right skills and ability. We discussed this in detail in our chapter on Training but it is a major issue time and time again and a major reason for the failure of programs.

It is essential that we use a robust and effective selection process for anyone who is going to have any role in leading and driving change in our business. We must pick our best people, not the people easy to spare. If we are going to make a difference, if we are going to see cultural and performance improvement, it is only logical to use your best people. Yes, this gives us problems around replacing them or backfilling their role for a few hours, days or weeks but we must find solutions to this issue.

9. Internal customers are sidelined

It's easy to remember the external customers, as for many businesses the motivation for Business Improvement is to improve quality. However, it is common to forget that customers are not limited to those who are buying a product or service. Internal customers are those who use a product or process within the company and everyone in the business must understand who their customers are (who uses my outputs from my activities) and what is important to them.

The more the business can become customer-focused on both internal and external customers the better. All activities, new products, new services, projects, decisions should all be viewed from a customer's perspective. As such, the voice of the customer becomes vital for everyone in the company to understand.

Many projects fail because they don't understand or take into account the voice of the customer when they are collecting data, analysing the situation or developing solutions. Even if the Green or Black Belt understand the importance and explain it to senior managers or sponsors, if they reject the concept or don't see the importance, they will not sign off the recommendations or agree with the scale of the problem. We must train and educate everyone in the business to see the importance of the voice of the customer.

10. Lack of process thinking

It becomes very difficult for anyone to truly implement Business Improvement if the company doesn't understand and buy into process thinking. Managers who don't start to focus on improving the whole process rather than just their functions will make it a real challenge for any Green or Black Belts to complete projects.

Organisations need to ensure that they understand and even reorganise their business around processes rather than functions. Eliminating functional thinking would be a major move forward when looking to implement Business Improvement. You might have to review structures, KPIs, roles and responsibilities as well as systems and procedures. The result will be improved business performance and customer and staff satisfaction levels.

11. Forcing solution to be found or implemented too quickly

One of the complaints we constantly get from Belts is that their manager is putting pressure on them to find a solution to a problem without them completing the DMAIC steps. Frustration is caused when a problem is allowed to continue as the Lean Six Sigma Belt insists that the root cause be found and then the process followed in full. This is, of course, correct but a good belt will put in either at the measure or analyse phase a temporary fix which will in effect stop the bleeding. This will then remove the immediate pressure from senior managers and will stop them from thinking that it takes a long time to solve a problem with Lean Six Sigma. The secret, however, is that the fix is only temporary and the Belt must continue to solve the problem to eliminate it. Too often, a Belt puts in a quick fix and the bleeding stops and they then forget about solving the root cause. The result is the problem comes back and people say, 'I told you that Lean Six Sigma doesn't work'.

Temporary fixes will provide space for all the data to be collected and solutions to be tested so that permanent solutions can be found. This requires not only a fully trained and supported Belt but also managers and sponsors who understand DMAIC and Lean Six Sigma. Champion and Sponsor training again become crucial to stop this from happening.

12. Green and Black Belts with limited experience

It takes strong technical knowledge, experience and analytical skills to run a successful project smoothly. It also takes change management and influencing skills to ensure that solutions are accepted and implemented fully. This is very difficult for many inexperienced Green or Black Belts.

Inexperience often manifests itself in the Define phase as Belts are unsure how to define the project tightly enough, leading to project spread and more time as complexity increases.

However, the Measure phase also presents challenges as it involves data collection, which is itself a mix of art and science to understand what information is, or will be, necessary to collect. As mentioned above, if the wrong data is collected, Belts may need to collect more data or, where this is not possible, will not be able to show the benefits and close the project.

In fact, in each of the phases of DMAIC, an inexperienced Green or Black Belt could make mistakes or take twice as long as required to figure out what to do and how to move forward. We often see this when projects are submitted for certification and every tool has been used as the Belt thought they had to use everything rather than realising that you use the tools required to move to the next stage.

Issues with time management, prioritising the project over other workloads, managing a team effectively and navigating any politics are also easier and quicker to overcome with a Belt who has had experience with them in the past. In a nutshell, the more projects you have run, the easier they become.

With your first groups of Green or Black Belts, it is essential that they are given support by sponsors but also by Master Black Belts. They can provide guidance and technical support as well as steer them in the right direction around all the softer skills needed for success. Investing in coaching and support from a Master Black Belt will ensure projects are completed and implemented successfully in a shorter time scale.

13. Limited support

One of the main underlying causes of problems with any Lean Six Sigma program is lack of support. Picking the wrong project, failing to collect the data required and getting sidetracked mid-way through a project are all issues that are easily overcome with the support and investment of senior stakeholders in the business.

Senior leaders can help pick a project that is relevant to the goals of the business and will therefore be given the time and resources it needs. Support from senior level will also ensure that Belts are not put under pressure to start a project before they have collected the data necessary to identify the root cause and prove benefits. In addition, managers are able to help newly qualified Belts who may struggle with areas such as smoothing out politics, selecting a good team and keeping a Belt focused on maintaining the momentum of the project.

A full suite of support needs to be put in place to help Belts, sponsors and the executives to deploy an effective change program and make Business Improvement a way of life. This might require hiring professionals but the investment will be worth it as projects are completed quicker and with greater success, providing a faster return of investment.

14. Not ensuring that the training is fit for purpose

Do you really need to spend 20 days in a classroom to train a Black Belt? Do you need to cover every tool in the toolbox, even though the delegate might never use them? As we discussed earlier in the book, it is essential that we design our training to suit our needs. Use blended learning to provide the best education and support for those being trained and don't be constrained by supposed experts in one approach or another.

Remember that lots of the tools taught in traditional approaches are not needed in a service environment or even in manufacturing so why teach them? Provide Master Black Belts to approach if they are needed or eLearning to take when required. As an example, Design of Experiments will be used by a small minority of delegates so what is the point of spending a day learning it? If you don't use a tool, you will forget it so it is a waste – the very thing we teach people to eliminate. All we need to do is give an overview of the tools so that people can recognise when they should use them and then a link to a Master Black Belt who can support them if they do need it.

We also need to ignore the supposed experts when it comes to what must be done or what must be used. Don't be told that you have to use this project charter or that storyboard format. Don't let people tell you there is only 1 way to use a tool; there are lots of ways to adapt a tool to suit your needs. Use what you have got, so if you have a project charter or project approval process already in place and you think it is fit for purpose, then use it.

We must also make the training relevant to the company and industry we are working in. Don't talk about cars or other manufacturing when training, coaching or working with a non-manufacturing company. Try to provide examples from the industry people work in. If you can't, then you should not be training Lean Six Sigma. We must make it relevant; we must be able to show how it can be used in your function or industry or market. This means that you can't just use a standard course with a standard script; it must be adapted to suit the needs of the audience. When we get to improve in the DMAIC process and we ask Green or Black Belts to present their project to influence those affected, we train them to adapt their presentations, so we should do the same.

Also, don't get hung up on what other companies say they do for training. Some say that projects have to save x pounds or dollars to count – this is of course total rubbish. Projects can be of any size. Why should a Green Belt have to save x or a Black Belt y? Every company has a different set of needs and opportunities. Set the goals relative to the possibilities inside a company. For some businesses, saving £10K is as good as saving £100K in another. We need to work with the company to understand how savings are calculated and what a success looks like.

15. Not certifying Green and Black Belts properly

Although we say that there should not be a set limit on what savings should be achieved to certify, it is in our opinion essential that you certify your people properly. If you don't, then people will realise that the qualification you are promising them is, in fact, meaningless for their résumé or CV.

As we suggested earlier in the book, to certify in the most effective manner, each Belt must attend the training, pass an end of course exam and most importantly, prove they can apply the learning through completion of a DMAIC project. At Green Belt level, 1 project and at Black Belt level, 2 projects. Each project should then be presented to the steering group or executives so they can appreciate what has been done and sign off the success of the team and the Green and Black Belt.

Proper certification in this way has many functions. Firstly, delegates can prove to others they have followed best practice certification. You have the opportunity to praise and thank teams and Belts for their hard work. You can also be sure that a robust process has been followed and a strategically important problem solved permanently. But also, you can use these projects as success stories with complete confidence that they are real. You will not be embarrassed or caught out.

Putting in a robust and 'Best in Class' certification process is essential for all concerned in Lean Six Sigma.

16. Not rewarding successes and failing to keep your best people

Many companies spend lots of time and money training, motivating and educating staff on the principle, tools and techniques associated with Lean Six Sigma. They invest time in allowing them to solve strategically important problems and saving the company lots of money, only to lose this talent quickly after certification.

Companies must realise that once trained as Green and, in particular, Black Belt, those involved become a valuable asset. Typically, these people become far more confident as they have learned to challenge management, they have been exposed to many levels above their pay grade in a company and they know how to speak with data. They also know they can save companies time and money while improving customer service. Not only that; they know how to prove that they have done so.

As a result, many Green and Black Belts start to demand more from their employers. They have upskilled so they expect to be recognised in some way. If they are not, they know they can take their talent elsewhere, where it will be recognised by promotions, pay rises, bonuses etc. We must ensure that we design into our company ways to ensure this doesn't happen. How will we reward success? How will we demonstrate that we value this newly skilled talent in our company? Failure to do so may well result in lost staff and force us to start the whole process again.

These are all ways to try and learn from others' mistakes and to ensure that our Lean Six Sigma program and projects are a success. However, this is one large area which we must also learn from and ensure we take into account when we are designing and deploying Business Improvement. We have mentioned many times the change management aspects. So let's now look at that in more detail.

Fundamental reason for Deployment failure

Any or all of the above will be contributing factors to why any program or deployment may fail. When designing our approach, we must learn from these reasons and ensure they don't occur in our approach. However, there is a fundamental reason for the failure of many programs. If you are one of the many companies that have tried unsuccessfully to implement any form of Business Improvement, then you will discover that the human aspect, the change management aspect, will be the root cause.

- You have not included your people
- You have not convinced your people
- You don't have the right leader or style of leadership
- You have not sold the benefits
- You don't understand how to implement change effectively

- Your systems and processes don't put your people at the heart of them
- You have not shown your people that change is possible
- You have not given your people security that they can make the change – reduced the fear

To put it succinctly, you have not influenced the people in your company that you have the vision, desire and ability to lead and make the change happen. You have not influenced them to understand why change is essential and that it will benefit them and the company. You have not influenced them to step out of their comfort zones and embrace the change.

If you truly want to influence people to embrace Business Improvement, then they must be able to answer the following 3 questions from their viewpoint. Not the businesses or your viewpoint but theirs. If they can answer these 3 questions positively, then they have a chance of your program or deployment succeeding. If they don't and there are enough people in your business who can't at all levels, then you will fail.

1. Do I understand the need for change?

2. Will it be worth it?

3. Can I do it?

Think about your last attempt to implement Business Improvement or any change for that matter. Could your people answer positively these 3 essential questions?

5.3 Understand how to implement change to be successful

Every manager in a business has to implement some kind of change at a certain point. As the 4th Industrial Revolution starts to really take hold with automation, robotics and drones, change is inevitable and people, and in particular managers, need to master implementing change quickly and effectively. Anyone who has ever had to implement change into a business understands how difficult and time consuming it is to make the change stick and be effective.

For over 30 years, I have been helping companies in every industry sector plan and implement change all over the world. Without a doubt, there is one key step that lays the foundation for successful change:

Ensure at least 75% of your staff understand why you have to make the change.

They don't have to agree with the reason to start with but they must understand why. Once you get over that hurdle, you can start to influence the other barriers to success but without it, you will keep getting people either verbally or mentally asking why.

Why do I believe that this is the vital first step to success? Most of us are quite happy with our current lives and what we are doing. We are in our comfort zones. Inside our comfort zone, we know what happens good or bad, we can plan for it, are not shocked by it and can accept it. As humans, we have enough to cope with and so we always take the easy option which will get us through the day with the least effort. As such, the way we do things day in, day out is comfortable and acceptable; it enables us to work on other things that we believe are more important. We don't have to focus on something new that means we have to put effort, thought and energy into, like changes at work. Taking the risk of doing new things or different things means we might disturb or equilibrium and as such, we don't want to engage in any change we don't have to.

All of this means that as managers, when we are faced with implementing change, no matter how small, we have an uphill journey on our hands. So, it is imperative that we get the first step right and build the foundations to ensure a successful change is implemented and accepted.

My experience has shown that some change is easier to implement than others. In a company that is in real trouble and everyone understands that and accepts it, they focus on the change as they know the dire consequences if they don't. This is why it is easier to make changes in failing companies than successful ones. People understand instinctively why management must do things in a different way.

In the majority of companies I work with and visit, however, this is not the case. The need for change, the sense of urgency associated with the change or the burning platform that you are facing is not obvious to all in the business. So when we ask people to do things in a different way, the first question they ask is why?

If you are going to ask me to do things differently, step out of my comfort zone and take a risk, if I can't answer the question of why, I will not engage, may resist or just become the silent mass who don't assist with the change process in the company. This leads to change stalling, taking longer or, at worst, not happening, despite the best effort of managers, which means a waste of all the time and money we have spent.

So how do you articulate the need for change?

When I work with senior management teams who are trying to

change the culture of an organisation or want to implement new systems or processes or new ways of working, I ask them to tell me the need for change or the sense of urgency for the change. I have lost count of the number of management teams who find it extremely difficult to explain to me in simple terms why they want to make the changes. Those that can articulate the need for change can only provide it from the perspective of senior managers. So, they talk about why the business must do this or that and explain it from their viewpoint.

If we want to get 75% of our people to understand why they must change, we must articulate it in a manner that they understand and believe in. They must appreciate the need to change in order to start to engage in the change process.

What can managers do to help communicate the need for change?

Firstly, position, communicate and explain the need for change from each group of people's perspectives. That means you can't use the same presentation and approach for everyone in the business as their worlds and what is important to them are different. You must invest in understanding your people, where the business is and what is vital to each person. This takes time and effort and is not just the development of a bland presentation.

If you understand what is happening and why from a number of different perspectives, then you can start to articulate it. I would suggest that you think about the following areas:

- Customers perspective
- The business performance perspective
- The markets perspective
- Your competitive position
- Your people's perspective – what is important to them

This would enable you to explain the change from all viewpoints.

Secondly, when you are explaining the need for change, you should articulate the consequences of not changing. This might mean that things are OK now but if we don't change, the competition will overtake you. It might mean that you go bust, it might mean that overtime is stopped or fewer people will be taken on, etc. This gives a view of the future to each group you have to convince to change.

Thirdly, you then have to be able to articulate the benefits of going through all of this change and turmoil and new ways of working or delivery. In other words, tell people what is in it for them.

Fourthly, what is your vision of the future? What will the world look like for them once the change has been implemented? You can explain this from each of the perspectives listed above.

Plan to obtain 75% of staff to understand the need for change.

Once we have developed the need for change, the next element is to ensure that everyone understands that need. This means setting up a communications plan to let people hear, digest, question and comment on that need. If we assume that just by telling them they will get it and buy into your well thought out arguments, then you are being a tad naive.

People need to hear the message a number of times, from different people. They need to believe what you are saying. They need to be given the time to ask questions and feel they are getting the truth back in return. They need to discuss it with friends and colleagues so that they can appreciate what is being said. They will then have more questions and demand more answers. After you have been through that process, you might find that they understand the need and with some luck, they will accept that need.

To do all of the above requires time and effort on your behalf. You need to plan communications, set up feedback loops, develop your delivery style and answer questions that people have not asked but are thinking. All of this means that you will typically need to have a person whose job it is to work on these elements. You will need charismatic presenters who are trusted and can influence others.

What you don't want to do is:

- Use one presentation for all
- Send different messages from different managers
- Use people who are poor at presenting just because they are in senior positions
- Don't ask for or react to feedback
- Provide no time for people to discuss the change
- Communicate last thing on a Friday
- Provide no real detail showing you have not thought it through
- Position it as a fait accompli
- Make demands

If you do, guess what: people will not work with you, help you and the whole thing will take longer and will probably not be a success.

Investing in these early stages of change pays massive benefits later on. It also shortens the whole process although at the start it will appear the opposite.

Why do managers struggle to explain the need for change to their staff?

To implement successful change, we need at least 75% of staff to understand why! Most companies struggle to get anywhere near that number of people to understand why they must step out of their normal day-to-day routines into a new and uncomfortable world.

When I work with senior management teams, they all want to implement some kind of change in their companies. New systems, new processes, changes to working practises and new cultures are just some of the changes they want to implement into their company. Most senior management teams have a reason for doing so: they want to increase productivity, improve customer service or increase profits, for example. Why then are so many changes in any business so difficult? Why do management teams find it so hard to explain to their staff the need for the change?

- Most of the time, staff are not aware of what is really going on inside and outside the company or with customers or product development – Happy talk
- Managers don't understand the reality of their own business – Gemba walk
- We don't understand what our people do, what they go through, what motivates them
- We can't communicate to the people in the correct way
- We only look at the world from our viewpoint

If we all agree that most people will take the easy option in life and that when asked to do something different this upsets their equilibrium and as such, are not keen to do so, then they must understand why to embrace any kind of change. If we do not communicate what is happening until it is too late, it is not surprising that they don't accept a change instantly. Most employees in most companies have no real clear view of what is happening in the company they work in. They don't know the financial situation, they don't understand the market and their competitors, they don't know what customers' demands are and how good we are at satisfying them. They don't understand the problems of the company or the issues it is facing. As managers, we normally do as we see reports, get presentations and have discussions about these things every day. So, when we are told that a change is needed, we normally understand quite quickly why. Others who are kept in the dark, however, don't have this background, perspective and knowledge so it will take them far longer to accept the need for change.

If you are a company that keeps people abreast with the list above, when you do come to implement a change, you are starting from a very much higher point than most. We would suggest that if you are moving into a period where you will need to implement change that you amplify the information given to staff so that they are ready. Review how and the amount of information you share with staff and you will be amazed at how little they are actually told.

We also come across some managers who can't articulate the real need for change in a business as they simply don't know what is really happening in their own businesses. In a small business, it is easy to keep on top of what is happening because you have to as there are so few of you. However, as you grow, you start to lose sight of the day-to-day activities. You become encased in your own function and don't know what is happening elsewhere. If the data and information provided to you as the top team are not sufficient or flawed, this can also have a major effect on your ability to know what is happening.

Before you embrace any change in a company, we would urge you to do some data collection, some diagnostics, some analysis to ensure you are starting from the right point. Spend some time in your business talking to people, understanding their problems, observing the operations in practice. This is called a Gemba walk – going to the shop or office floor and understanding each part from the perspective of what really happens.

A surefire killer for any change program is where there is a disconnect between what management thinks and the reality in the business. You will communicate the need for change but it will not resonate with the staff as that is not what they experience on a day-to-day basis. The result is a lack of understanding and a slowdown in the whole process.

To explain the need for change and get people to understand it, you must communicate from the perspective of your staff at each level or area in the business. If, however, you don't understand your staff, how can you do that? You must understand what motivates and concerns them. You must understand what they do on a day-to-day basis. You must understand what they go through each day. Only then can you start to position the change in a way that they will understand; only then will you be able to show how the change will help them.

To do this, you must spend time with your people. Leaders understand their people, they talk to them, they observe and support them. Managers tell them what to do. Every person in your business will have a different motivation for doing their job – you must work out what it is. I worked with a major Telecoms company in a call centre. They wanted to implement change but their problem was that if the call centre down the road increases the hourly rate by just 1 penny, they lose staff. This told us that pay was the major motivation as basic needs were not being met. Trying to implement cultural change without addressing this first was impossible.

Gemba walks will provide you with some understanding of what they do but spend a day in the life of your people, experience what they experience and then you will understand the world from their perspective. Do they have the right tools, are conditions good enough, do they get support? Find out and then you can start to influence the need for change.

If you don't understand the motivations of your people or what they go through, you can only present the need for change from the positions you do know, which is yours or the businesses, and there are far more people not in management positions to convince than are.

Another area where managers fail to explain the need for change to their staff is that they can't communicate. If you can't communicate in a style which your people understand, then you can't communicate with them. If you use data, graphs, boring presentations and complex words and that doesn't meet the style and needs of your people, you will not be able to get your message across. Many management teams don't know how to communicate with their staff. They don't do it regularly, they have no relationship or rapport with them and then can't adapt to the needs of their teams.

Leaders, managers and change managers need to be exceptional communicators and presenters both in one-to-one situations but also in group situations. Most are not. You need to get the timing right, the feedback mechanism right, the tone right, answer un-asked questions, show you understand their world and the impact this will have. You need to use the right language, the right style and the right words. You need to plan it, adapt it and change it to suit your audience and you need to listen to the feedback. Most managers don't spend any time doing this; they just use 1 presentation and stand up and wing it. We then wonder why it doesn't convince people.

The key to any communication is to put yourself in the shoes and world of those listening to the presentation. If you can't see the world and understand the world from their perspective, then you can't do this. This is why you must spend time understanding your people.

It is crucial that we convince 75% of people of why the change is needed. Managers need to spend time understanding their business, their people and then plan how they will articulate and communicate this to their teams or you will not be as successful as you could be.

If you don't believe that 75% of staff need to understand the need for change, just think about some of the improvements you have tried to make and if they were successful or not. When you say we will do X, Y or Z, do they get done with no problems exactly as you wish or do they take a long time to get implemented? My guess is they take a long time, get diluted and a lot fail to get completed at all. This is due to the lack of understanding by those affected to understand the need for change. Whether it is a small change in a department or a company-wide change, 75% of those affected must as a first step understand why. Only then can we start to work on the next 2 key areas:

- Will it be worth it?

- Can I do it?

Spend some time and reflect on these areas. Do you struggle to convince people to change because you don't actually understand your business and your people? Do you plan your communications and interactions or just wing it? Reflect on these areas and you might find a way to make your next change more effective.

5.4 Senior Executive and Managers must change first to implement change successfully – It is all down to you

Every major change in a business needs leaders who display the right behaviour, have the correct understanding and are willing to commit to it. Your staff must have an awareness of the change, an understanding of why you need to change or a clear burning platform. It all starts by getting 75% of people to understand why. Why must we do something differently? Why must I experience the pain, risk, time-consuming activities to do things in a different way? Why must I invest time, effort, mental power and thought into doing a new thing? And it all starts with senior managers who want the change in the first place. If you can't change, why should anyone else?

Too many senior managers expect others to implement change in their business while they don't change. I am not talking about changing their behaviour to the desired change they wish others to adhere to. I am talking about changing the way they implement change in their business.

Most senior managers try to implement change in the same way, with as little impact on them as possible but maximum impact on others.

If you want to implement change, you will have to invest time, effort and most importantly, learn how to implement it effectively. If you don't, you will get the same results that you always have.

Why is it that change is slow or not possible in your business? We always blame others for resisting or people for not understanding but the real reason is we didn't do it right. We need to change the way we try to implement change and we need to invest significant time into making the change happen.

Why is it that getting a senior management team in a room for a few days to train them, teach them or help them is so hard? We are too busy, we are too important, we already understand what is needed? If so, then why do all your changes not just happen?

Think about the last major change you wanted to implement in your business. Did it go well, did it work, did you obtain the benefits you set out to obtain? In general, the answer to these questions is 'we got nowhere near the benefits we planned, it took far longer than we thought, it was a real effort, we gave up'. These are the common responses if you are being honest.

If you are going to implement change in your business, you need to understand how to do so effectively. To implement change effectively, you are going to have to make it a priority, spend lots of time working on it, communicate 5 to 7 times the same message, convince your people at each level why they must change and drive the desire into them. You are going to have to spend lots of time working on and supporting the change, which will mean spending less time on other activities.

Normally, when senior managers make a decision to implement a change in their business, they might spend some time determining what it should be. They might spend time understanding where they are and what needs to happen. They then normally hand over the responsibility to a program manager, a project manager, a change manager or a trusted member of staff. If these people are lucky, they will get the odd appearance at an event and then they will be quizzed about progress by the senior management team. Does that sound like how you implement change?

Virtually any significant change that is successful in an organisation needs so much more from their leaders and senior managers. Every expert, every change model and, my vast experience says, senior managers must engage, dedicate time and effort and adapt their behaviours for it to be a sustained success. That means that senior managers must change their attitude to how they implement change first for it to be a success.

They must develop the awareness and understanding of why the change is needed in at least 75% of their staff. They must conduct ongoing discussions, hold one-to-one chats, have regular communications, attend workshops, support those designing and deploying the change. All of this takes time and effort and, in most cases, new skillsets. If you are determined as a senior manager to make significant changes in your business, you must start to lead rather than manage. You must change your approach to change and you must lead by example.

What's in it for me?

If for whatever reason, I think that all the extra work, learning new skills or processes and stepping out of my comfort zone will be more hassle than it is worth, I will resist the change, no matter which level I am in a company. It might be that you can force people to adhere to your new ways of working but you will not win their hearts. Remember that we are trying to change the culture in the organisation so we need hearts and minds, not just compliance.

As such, it is vital that everyone at every level can work out for themselves if it will be worth it. For some, it might mean keeping their job, for others increased responsibility. It might make their lives easier, it might mean learning new skills; the secret is that each person will answer the question in a different way. We, as executives and managers, must influence them to understand the benefits and work out that this change will make things better for them personally.

To do this, managers must have the ability to influence. There are loads of books and training courses on how to improve your influencing skills and we would recommend that every manager works on this skillset. You need to become highly effective at selling the benefits of your change and how it will impact each group or individual in your company. As mentioned earlier, this is not easy and will require time and effort but the rewards are massive.

What kind of things might make people answer positively to the questions of if it will be worth it? You need to know and work with your people but some answers might be personal, others for their team and others for their company, or more likely a combination of all 3. Let's look at some options:

POTENTIAL BENEFIT AREAS

To You

- Career progression.
- Increase in recognition (internally).
- Better working environment.
- Improved professional satisfaction.
- Increased awareness of where I fit in and how I contribute.
- Increased clarity for personal development.
- Increased technical expertise.
- Certification.
- Less hassle at work.
- Less oversight by managers.

- Inspired by being part of a high-performance service.
- Greater sense of 'team'.
- Improved kudos.

- You can rely on the team to give you the best technical advice.
- Enhanced rewards.
- Closer working relations.

To Your Team

To Your Organisation
- Increased profits.
- Products would be more reliable.
- Business has the support resource where it is most effective.
- Higher industrial profile.
- Greater recognition from DB (dynamic structure/forward-thinking/meeting requirements).
- "Jewel in Crown" ideas from management.
- Higher prestige.

I am sure you can add lots more reasons why people might say yes. In effect, we must sell our vision. We must get people to buy in themselves to what we are saying so that they can answer the question of if it will be worth it. You might have to think like a salesperson. Think about your vision; what are the features, advantages and benefits of what we are doing from each group's viewpoint? You then need to influence them all. As stated above, this means you spending time and effort working to get buy-in. It will mean using different approaches and different channels each time you communicate or engage with people in your organisation. In other words, you need to be a great influencer

HOW TO SELL THE BENEFITS

 Features
These are built into your idea or suggestion – timing, costs, resources and so on. They will remain locked up in your idea whether the person agrees or not.

 Benefits
These are far more important. They translate features into exiting statements which clearly show how others will gain.

 Advantages
These are the comparative benefits. For example, more money, greater savings, easier life, faster.

Features are one of the easier things to identify. These are facts or characteristics of your business, products, and services. For example, a "1-inch insulation layer" on a sleeping bag is the feature.

Advantages are what the features do. These tend to be factual, and aren't connected to a prospect need… yet. For example, "it helps retain body heat on cold nights," (sticking with our sleeping bag example).

Benefits answer why someone should value the advantage. It connects the facts about your product to a solution for your client. For example, "when you're camping, you'll have a nice warm sleep at night so that when you wake up, you'll be well-rested and ready for a day of fun activities."

To be a great influencer, first we need to understand what makes a great influencer, what influence is. Influencing is about understanding yourself and the effect or impact you have on others. Though on occasion it can be one way, the primary relationship is two way, and it is about changing how others perceive you.

In other words, the cliché perception is reality makes perfect sense in the context of influencing.

It doesn't matter what's going on internally for you - if it isn't perceived by the other person, then it doesn't exist other than in your mind.

Influencing is about being able to move things forward, without pushing, forcing or telling others what to do.

Amazingly people with great influencing skills draw people to them. People like being around them as they typically have great energy. They don't just sit around; they make things happen and we are drawn to people who get things done and are positive. Great influencers get on with it and don't moan and groan.

To influence well, you must start by understanding yourself and the effect you have on others. You must review and think about what happens and why, constantly be looking for feedback so that you can improve. Influencing is about changing the way people perceive you so you can have an effect on them. So, no matter how bad a day you are having, you can't let it show; concentrate on the other person and make it happen.

If you study what makes people great influencers, you can discover some patterns and common themes:

- They can sell the benefits of their ideas
- They can neutralise resistance, preferably in advance
- They find different ways to influence different people
- They listen attentively to what others say
- They can identify what people's needs and wants are so they know what buttons to press
- They are very good at being empathetic
- They have the ability to notice how people respond
- They are exceptional at building and maintaining rapport
- They don't use weak language
- They are enthusiastic
- They plan and rehearse
- We believe in them

What makes us believe in them is also an interesting area to explore and understand. Below is a list of some elements associated with what makes us believe in another person. You tend to find that you believe a person if they speak with data. It answers questions, it shows that some thought has gone into it and that they understand what is happening. It gives you confidence that you have done your homework and put in some effort. This only works if you look the part and act the part based on what you expect the person to be like. If you trust and respect a person, they will build rapport with you and you are more likely to believe them. If you can sell a vision, paint a picture of the future and make it sound good, look good, then they will believe. If you can almost mesmerise them with the way you tell the story or demonstrate the future, you can get people to follow you. If you have enabled them to be part of the vision or the process, then they will join in. If you tell people the same thing over and over again, they will eventually start to believe the message. Ultimately, people love positive energetic people so use passion and energy and we can get people to believe and you can influence them.

What makes us believe in others:

- Speaking with data
- Professional approach
- We like them, trust them and respect them. We have a rapport with them
- We want to believe them as they sell the vision
- We are mesmerised by them
- You have included them or consulted them
- They repeat the same message over and over
- They have enthusiasm and passion

As managers, executives, owners and leaders, we need to develop our influencing skills. We need to understand what motivates each person or each group of people we work with. If we do we can tailor our approach to influence them. As such, you need to understand and use different influencing strategies and approaches. You need to understand that you can influence the following areas and how to use them to be effective. Spend time investigating and understanding each of these areas and how you can use them to influence.

- Physiology
- Language
- Credibility
- Actions and behaviour
- Position
- Friendship/relationships
- Reciprocation
- Socially
- Scarcity
- Environment
- Motivation
- Desirability
- Team environment
- Peers

Great influencers are typically great at communication, interpersonal relationships, presenting, being assertive and being attentive to others. They use their skills in some instances without even knowing they have them to get things done. This is exactly what we want our leaders, change agents and Lean Six Sigma Belts to become.

Can I do it?

The last questions leaders must get people to answer for themselves is, "Can I do it?" I might understand why we need to change, I might convince myself that it would be worth it to me to do so but if I have fear or apprehension that I can't do it, I will not engage and make it happen. This is an area we all too often ignore. We think that just telling people to do it and get on with it will be enough. Once again, spending time designing how you will support people to answer this question and then supporting them as they learn new skills will pay massive dividends as we change our culture.

There are lots of different ways to help people feel they can achieve a new skill, behaviour or approach:

- Create confidence in others that they can with great influencing skills
- Inspire them with examples of those like them who have succeeded before them
- Tell them a story: use the art of storytelling to gain their support
- Practice safely: create a safe environment where trials can take place
- Let them design it
- Persuade with peer pressure

One of the ways to give people confidence that they can do something is to show them others doing the same tasks or demonstrating new behaviours. If we can watch and talk to people we think are just like us, then we will be convinced. The people they see must be similar in background, attitudes and values as them so that they believe that they are the same. If you want to show people that a change is good, take them to see people like them but make sure you plan the visit. Lots of people do benchmark but in effect, they just go to another company for a tour. This will not really help although it is better than nothing. The best visits are planned and allow the people to see and speak to those who have the behaviour you are trying to instil. It might be that this can be done internally by visiting another site or department or it might mean trying to set up an external visit. Just remember that nothing will convince people like seeing others doing the new behaviour.

If you can't show people the new behaviour being done by people like those we are trying to influence, we need to find another way to influence them. A powerful story can transport people into the new world you are trying to obtain. This requires a well-constructed and vivid story that takes people to a new place.

If we examine influential speeches that have had a profound effect on those who hear them, we discover some common themes. Here is a very small list of powerful speeches that have had major effects on the world and I am sure you can think of others.

- Martin Luther King – I have a dream
- Winston Churchill – Fight on beaches
- John F Kennedy – My fellow Americans

As change agents, we are not expecting you to be Martin Luther King but we can gain some understanding by examining what makes a good story. If, however, you can take your people on a journey that paints the picture of what the new process will be like or the new way of working will make them feel, you can start to influence them to believe they can do it.

When you develop your story, tell them everything; the good, the bad and the ugly. Ensure that you paint the picture of the new behaviour and why you need to change and how you know they will be able to do it.

A well-told story:

- Gives an understanding: A powerful story can change people's points of view by presenting the new process in a clear way. It shows the cause and effect of the new flow, in a consequence-free environment.
- Is listened to: If a story is told well, people will take time away from thinking about their own arguments for resistance and will listen.
- Is motivating: The language and delivery of a story can create an emotional connection to the need for change.

Another way to allay fears is to let people practice and participate in safety. Seeing a person handle a snake is not the same as handling one. So, if you want to overcome a fear of snakes, eventually you have to touch one. If we can let people try out a new process in a trial or pilot then they can see what it is like and they can get confidence that they can do it. Ensure you set it up correctly and that failing is not a problem as it is a practice. Let them make mistakes, get used to new processes or equipment or systems, give them training and support and you will get more confident people. The last thing you want to do is have loads of management standing over the person as they try to gain confidence; leave them alone and let them get on with it. Let them talk to colleagues and most of all, listen to feedback and act on it. If people are involved, they will be more likely to change.

As in sport, practice makes perfect, not just any old practice but deliberate practice, which is supported and provides feedback frequently and quickly without reprisals if people make mistakes. If we enable people to break down tasks and try it a small bite at a time, they will see it is all possible. The old adage of 'Eat the elephant one bite at a time' is totally true; have mini-goals and you will enable people to change behaviours.

You can also use others to convince people they can do it. When a respected individual attempts a new behaviour and succeeds, this one act alone can go further in motivating others to change than anything else. But only if they are respected at that time. They can convince people they can succeed, they can influence people to change behaviours and they make amazing advocates for change.

The secret is to find them. Most of the time, it is obvious who people look up to in an organisation but if not, ask them who is the best, the most experienced person who takes the lead and others will tell you. If we get them to start telling people that the new way is great, then change can be affected. If you include them in the design of your solution or new processes, they will become advocates.

You can also convince people that they can do it themselves by allowing them to work in teams or with friends. Whatever you need to do, work on your strategy to enable people to convince themselves they can do it.

5.5 Change your focus to implement change

As you have seen, to implement Business Improvement successfully, we as managers, owners, leaders and change agents need to change our focus to ensure success. To implement a change in a business requires 2 fundamental elements: a good solution (implementing a new Business Improvement Culture) to the problem and people to accept and use the new solution. Unfortunately, in business, we spend all of our time on only one of these elements – the good solution.

We send time, effort and money on designing our structure, processes, training our people in technical skills and virtually no time thinking about how to influence people, how to engage, understanding our staff, communicating, obtaining feedback, adapting our approach, etc.

In reality, most solutions are not that complicated. Whether it is the solution to why we miss deadlines, how to reduce costs or how to improve quality, the reality is that once you understand some tools and techniques, follow DMAIC, involve the right people and have experience, then the solutions are straight forward. The difficult part is the acceptance by your staff. However, we place all of our resources and effort on the other part of the equation.

As businesses, we need to change our emphasis and our focus. Spend time planning our deployment, spend time understanding our people, spend time learning the skills of influence and communication and use the right people to make that happen. Remember; just because you're the CEO or MD of a company, you might not be the right person to lead and drive the change. You need to give your complete and unerring support but you might not have the charisma or ability to lead the change. For any CEO to understand this and admit it is a major strength, not a weakness. Anyone who has this level of self-awareness has great strength.

We must think differently, act differently and put different emphasis on our deployment.

Do I understand it? Awareness – 75% of your people affected by your change must understand why the change you are looking to implement is needed. This starts with your senior management group and then works downwards in the organisation as each level must provide support to the next in terms of developing awareness.

Build the desire for the change – If people are going to change the way they do things, act or behave, they must have a desire to do so. We must develop the desire from the top to the bottom of the organisation as again, each level will support building the desire in the next level. Create and share the vision

Understand the change in detail – Once we have the change, we must communicate it so that people can assess if their desire for the solution matches the solution that has been developed.

Will it be worth it? – Each individual must then assess if the effort to accept the change will be worth it. We must support people to understand that the solution will be worth it to them personally. If they can't answer the questions of if it will be worth it to them personally positively, then they will not change or will resist the change.

Can I do it – Even if a person thinks it will be worth it, if they believe they can't do it, they will not accept and embrace the change. We must provide the confidence they can do it so that they can take the next step of learning new skills, approaches or behaviours. Show them how they will be supported through this stressful time

Build the ability – After convincing yourself you can do something, you need to build your ability with the new task, behaviour or approach. We need to support our people through the change, provide them safe ways to practise, ensure that they are given help when needed to accept the new working methods, behaviours or requirements

Reinforce the change – Ensuring the change becomes the new norm and part of their comfort zone requires them to be given reinforcement and encouragement as they progress. We must constantly provide reinforcement, support and celebrate success

This side of the equation is made difficult by the fact that we are dealing with people. Every person in your business is motivated differently, looks at the world differently, has different histories and abilities. Each person will need individual support through change. That takes time and effort. However, if we work on this side of the equation, change will have a far greater chance of success.

Why then do people only concentrate on one side of our equation? Simple – it's easier. Solving problems is typically what we like and have been trained to do from an early age. As a result, as managers, we come up with a solution and then more or less say get on with it. We are then surprised when it doesn't work. We have not put any time into communicating the need, developing a desire, demonstrating what is in it for them, proving that and then supporting people so they can do it.

All of this takes time, is a different skillset and is difficult to measure. Very few people go on real change management training and even less of us practise it. We don't have time, we just want the solution implemented and, in a world that requires more and more instant gratification, this will be a problem. However, real and lasting solutions to problems that work will take time and a new structure as well as new thought patterns from senior managers.

We must work on both sides of the equation at the same time. The earlier you start to engage people the better, as we all know. At the same time as setting up your project-solving team, also set up a change management team. They may be the same people but set them up with change management activities as well as problem-solving activities. As an example, while you are defining your project, also carry out a stakeholder analysis so you know who has to be influenced and communicated to, how big the challenge will be and what some of the issues may be. While collecting data, set up a communications strategy so that senior managers are delivering small group awareness sessions, etc.

You will discover that the change management side of our equations takes more effort from sponsors and senior managers. It may involve HR and communications. It will take more time from the organisation but remember that this is the side that will make the solution a reality. Without this effort, you may design the perfect solution but if nobody uses it, then it was a waste of time.

There is also, however, a third element to successful change being implemented into an organisation and that is how you organise and implement change in your business. People like Kotter have been studying this for decades and by learning structures like this, you can focus on the right areas to be successful.

As senior managers, it is vital that we change the way in which we try to influence and organise change in our businesses. We must not just focus on the solution but also the implementation of the solution and the structure in which we will implement it. We must dedicate time, effort and resources to the change as well as the solution.

Section 6

Conclusions and next steps

6.1 Conclusions

For many companies, Business Improvement in its numerous guises has been tried many times, for others, you are just setting out on your journey. No matter your situation, you will now realise that Business Improvement is vital to company prosperity and success, no matter your industry or competitive position.

There is no standard way to design and deploy your program. There is no silver bullet that if you apply over a 6-month period, you will arrive at eutopia. Every business is different due to its history, culture, people and goals. Senior Managers, Owners, Leaders and executives must invest time into understanding Business Improvement, designing your approach and most importantly, how they will implement this major change in their business.

It is not enough for you to send others on a training course, to hire a Master Black Belt or to pass on responsibility to one of your team. You must embrace the fact that this kind of change starts with you. You must understand, you must change behaviour, you must change your focus for this to be a success. Yes, you can obtain some fantastic outcomes by letting people in your organisation certify as Green or Black Belts and solve problems using the approach but you will not engage all of your staff and change the culture.

If you truly wish to have a vision for your company where each person identifies problems or issues every day, generates possible solutions and then implements them, then you must design your approach to make that happen.

For decades, I have watched companies try to achieve the goal of total engagement and the development of a Business Improvement culture. Most have failed for all of the reasons listed in this book. They focus on the wrong elements, they have a very poor understanding of what Business Improvement is and how to implement it but most of all, they don't put in the effort in the right places.

For your organisation to be a success, we would strongly encourage you to spend time at the start of your journey planning and convincing your staff of the need for change. Invest in detailed and effective communications that will be used throughout your change program. Allow change managers to spend time working on the people aspects of the change rather than just the technical ones. You, as a manager, executive, etc. must become more engaged and start to influence day in, day out. You must walk the talk; you must change your behaviour to show you are totally committed.

Make sure your senior management team has the same commitment and understanding of why you are changing. Develop your shared vision and then start the process of influencing.

Don't fall for the same mistakes that others have, but learn from their setbacks. This might even start with the name you call your change. Does it matter what you call it? Not really, as long as you are consistent, you all have a common understanding and there are no negative connotations associated with it. For me, I don't care if you call it Business Improvement, Continuous Improvement, Operational Excellence, Lean Six Sigma, Lean or even George. It's about designing a program that will work for you. It's about supporting your people and it's about cultural change.

Imagine in a years' time; virtually everyone in your business identifies issues and solves them. Just imagine what that would do to your bottom line, your customer satisfaction and your staff satisfaction. Imagine the way people would talk, how they would make decisions, how they would focus on processes, how the customer would be at the heart of everything you do, how everything would be better quality and safer. How good would it be to make that cultural change?

Follow the steps outlined in this book but also invest time in learning other skills, how to influence, how to motivate, how to understand yourself and others. The payback will be incredible.

Thank you for reading this book and I hope that we have managed to make you think, challenge the norm and give you some ways to improve your business. Now that you have completed the book, we would invite you to certify as a Lean Six Sigma Champion. Simply follow the steps outlined below and you can prove you are a certified Lean Six Sigma Champion.

1. Go to the Leadership page of the website www.100pcEffective.com/leadership
2. Click Training Login
3. Create an account and verify your email address
4. Then login and you will be able to take the Lean Six Sigma Champion exam and certify
5. Pass the exam and you will be able to download your certificate

I wish you the best of luck with changing your culture. If you require any support, then please get in touch with me. I love to hear about how people are transforming their organisation and if I can help, just let me know.

Thank you.

Acknowledgements

Many people have helped to make this book a reality. It has been several years in the writing, with contributions from members of the 100% Effective team, clients, colleagues and delegates on numerous training courses, all of whom have provided me with insight, thoughts and inspiration.

I would particularly like to thank my wife Sharon and my children for all their support and encouragement during the writing process. I would also like to thank Gemma Nunn, who has done an amazing job developing the images you will see throughout the book. Wendi Ellis has provided me with advice and support during the editing and publishing process and her help has been invaluable in completing this project. Chris Jarrett, Mike Titchen and Grace Henderson have also been an integral part of the team so a massive thanks to them as well.

Writing a book about how to lead and implement business improvement successfully takes years of working with amazing clients. Each time we train or support a delegate or company, we learn something new. Over the last 30 years, understanding what works and what doesn't has enabled me to write this book and without everyone I have worked with, it would not have been possible. So, a massive thanks to anyone I have ever worked with throughout my career.

I will keep learning, no matter the client, person being supported or company I give advice to. There is no one solution to implementing business improvement; you must adapt to your circumstances and needs and as a result, we are all students and must keep learning and changing to ensure success.

ABOUT THE AUTHOR

John Wellwood

John Wellwood is an international Lean Six Sigma and Business Improvement specialist, who has worked for over 30 years across five continents as both a consultant, trainer, coach and practitioner.

Passionate about Change and Improvement, John has delivered seminars at the British Library, The Lean Six Sigma World Conference, Universities and countless events all over the world. His style of practical, simple and energetic delivery, along with his obsession to obtain results and educate, has given him a reputation as a change agent in the industry.

John established 100% Effective Ltd in 1999; a marketing leading firm that provides quality, support and innovation to the Business Improvement world. 100% Effective offers truly blended learning, designed to provide clients with bespoke, practical and effective training, coaching and consultancy.

His personal learning, amassed over 30 years, had given him a unique insight into how to implement and succeed in Business Improvement. Learn from others' mistakes, learn from a person with unquestionable credentials, learn from a person with true passion and understanding for implementing a Business Improvement Culture into your organisation.

SOURCES

- John P. Kotter, Leading change, Harvard Business Review Press, (2012)

- R. vickers, J. Field, C. Melakoski, Media Culture 2020: Collaborative Teaching and Blended Learning Using Social Media and Cloud-Based Technologies

- J. Young, Six Sigma Forum Magazine - November 2001

Printed in Great Britain
by Amazon

3963R00142